May 2000

Dear Mom

Happy Mothers Day!

Thanks for teaching me to "Be of Good Cheer" and the value of having a positive attitude. It has been a value that every other one can be based on.

I love you very much. You are the best mom any one could have.

Chris

1

To Make Ready a People

LUKE 1

The New Testament centers around Jesus and the infinite atonement that he lovingly wrought in our behalf. Sometimes, because of the great power and teachings of the Savior, the important mission of John the Baptist is overlooked.

The so-called covenant people of Jesus' day were in no way prepared for the coming of the Lord. They had wandered far from the teachings and commandments of the holy prophets and had written their own creeds and doctrines. The Jewish leaders had divided the people into groups and sects that were bitterly antagonistic toward one another. The rulers and priests served themselves more than they served God and the people. Priestcraft, self-righteousness, and wickedness characterized the leadership of the Jewish church. No wonder John the Baptist was referred to as a "voice . . . crying in the wilderness" (Luke 3:4) as he reintroduced the light of the gospel in this environment of apostasy and darkness.

John the Baptist prepared a small but humble group of believers so that the Savior's ministry would be more effective. The formal ministry of Jesus lasted only three short years, so it was vital to have a group of men and women who were ready to accept him as the Messiah and receive instruction and training from him.

John was born to Zacharias and Elisabeth even though they were both "stricken in years" (Luke 1:7). Elisabeth was barren, but like Sarah and Hannah of old, she became the recipient of a miracle from the Lord.

Both Zacharias and Elisabeth were of priestly descent through the lineage of Aaron, and Zacharias was a priest of the course of Abia. A thousand years before, David had divided the priests into twenty-four courses, and these courses took turns serving in the temple. Twice each year for a period of eight days each time, they lived in the temple and fulfilled their priestly duties. The course of Abia served in the Hebrew equivalent of April and October.

The priestly duties were diverse, so the priests drew lots to determine their individual assignments and duties for their eight days of service. Their duties included such things as burning morning and evening incense; setting out the shewbread for the week; slaying, cutting up, and sacrificing animals on the altar; trimming the seven lamps of the sacred golden candlestick; caring for the fire on the great temple altar; and removing the ashes of the sacrifices. The one duty desired above all others was to burn incense on the altar of incense in the Holy Place, which was the room next to the Holy of Holies. To keep the incense burning on this sacred altar was the high point of a priest's service. Since duty assignments were determined by lot, a priest would usually have this privilege very infrequently, if at all.

On this particular occasion, as lots were drawn by the priests the Lord guided the drawing so that Zacharias was assigned to minister in the Holy Place. As he sprinkled the incense on the burning coals, the ascending smoke and odor represented the prayers of all Israel. While Zacharias prayed within the Holy Place for the coming of the Messiah and for deliverance from sin, a multitude of people stood outside praying for the same thing.

Zacharias's prayer was answered in a marvelous and miraculous manner when the angel Gabriel appeared to him and told him that his prayer for the coming of the Messiah would soon be answered. Zacharias was told that his wife, Elisabeth, would have a son whom they should name John. This son would go before the Savior "to make ready a people prepared for the Lord" (Luke 1:17).

The fact that it was the angel Gabriel who appeared emphasizes the importance of the mission of John the Baptist. Only two angels are mentioned by name in the Bible: Michael, who was

Adam, and Gabriel, who was Noah. Michael is next to Jesus and Gabriel is next to Michael in priesthood authority (see Joseph Fielding Smith, comp., *Teachings of the Prophet Joseph Smith* [Salt Lake City: Deseret Book Co., 1977], p. 157).

When Zacharias heard the promises of the as yet unidentified angel, they seemed too wonderful to be true, so he asked, "Whereby shall I know this? for I am an old man, and my wife well stricken in years" (Luke 1:18). The angel responded by introducing himself and bearing testimony that he came from the presence of God and was speaking under God's direction. He then told Zacharias that, because of his hesitancy in accepting the angel's words, he would be struck dumb until the words were fulfilled. This not only demonstrated to Zacharias that Gabriel came with power but gave a forceful visual confirmation to the Jewish people that something extraordinary had taken place in the temple.

While these events were transpiring inside the temple, the people were waiting for Zacharias to come out of the Holy Place and pronounce the Aaronic blessing. They were marvelling that he tarried so long in the temple. When he came out and could not speak, they "perceived that he had seen a vision" (Luke 1:22). Thus the miraculous promises made in the temple were quickly dispersed throughout the land of Israel.

Elisabeth soon conceived and went into seclusion. When she was in her sixth month, she was visited by Mary, who had recently conceived the Son of God. Not only were Mary and Elisabeth relatives but, knowing that Elisabeth was carrying the forerunner to Christ, Mary must have wanted to share the news that she was going to be the mother of the Messiah. Together they could discuss the astonishing and wonderful events that were transpiring in their lives.

No sooner did Mary greet Elisabeth than John leaped in Elisabeth's womb and the Holy Ghost witnessed to her that Mary was carrying the Son of God. Together they rejoiced in the goodness of the Lord and marvelled that the Lord had found them worthy to bear such important sons. Mary visited with Elisabeth for about three months, so she may not have returned home until after the birth of John.

When John was eight days old, his family and friends met together to circumcise him and give him his name. The people wanted to name him Zacharias after his father, but Elisabeth said that he should be called John. As soon as Zacharias wrote that the name should be John, Zacharias's "mouth was opened immediately, and his tongue loosed, and he spake, and praised God" (Luke 1:64).

These miracles were done openly so that the Jewish people would know that something important was taking place among them. Luke writes that "all these sayings were noised abroad throughout all the hill country of Judea. And all they that heard them laid them up in their hearts, saying, What manner of child shall this be!" (Luke 1:65–66.)

The hand of the Lord was with John, and he grew and "waxed strong in spirit" (Luke 1:80). He readied himself so that he would be qualified to "go before the face of the Lord" (Luke 1:76) and prepare a people to be ready to accept the Savior. What an example John is to the young people of our day! He didn't wait until his mission years were upon him to prepare himself but sought and obtained the Spirit while he was young.

Because of his spiritual preparation, John spoke with great power and inspiration and became a powerful preacher for righteousness. Many people responded to his message of repentance and were baptized for a remission of their sins.

Latter-day revelation states, "Almost all men, as soon as they get a little authority, as they suppose, . . . immediately begin to exercise unrighteous dominion" (D&C 121:39). This was not the case with John the Baptist, for he demonstrated modesty and humility throughout his life. Referring to the Savior, John said, "[He who is] coming after me is preferred before me, whose shoe's latchet I am not worthy to unloose" (John 1:27).

When Jesus approached him to be baptized, John unpretentiously declared, "I have need to be baptized of thee, and comest thou to me?" (Matthew 3:14.) The next day, instead of resenting the fact that he would soon lose his following and the associated power and glory that many lesser men would desire, he pointed out Jesus to Andrew and John the Beloved and said to them, "Behold the Lamb of God!" When the two disciples heard this testimony, they left John and followed Jesus. (See John 1:36–37.)

Just before John was cast into prison, he was baptizing near Salim. Some of his disciples said unto him, "Rabbi, he that was with thee beyond Jordan, to whom thou barest witness, behold, the same baptizeth, and all men come to him." They may have been expecting John to show some jealousy or resentment, but instead he bore witness of the Savior by saying: "A man can receive nothing, except it be given him from heaven. Ye yourselves bear me witness, that I said, I am not the Christ, but that I am sent before him." He then told of the joy that he felt to be worthy to be associated with Jesus and declared, "He must increase, but I must decrease." (See John 3:23–30.)

John approached his calling with such dedication and humility that it is no wonder that Jesus said of him, "Among them that are born of women there hath not risen a greater than John the Baptist" (Matthew 11:11). Because of his willingness to prepare a people for the Lord, many were ready to accept the gospel and become the leaders of the Church of Jesus Christ.

Like John, each of us has been given the responsibility to prepare God's children for the coming of Christ. President Ezra Taft Benson declared:

> For nearly six thousand years, God has held you in reserve to make your appearance in the final days before the Second Coming of the Lord. Every previous gospel dispensation has drifted into apostasy, but ours will not. True, there will be some individuals who will fall away; but the kingdom of God will remain intact to welcome the return of its head—even Jesus Christ. . . . The final outcome is certain—the forces of righteousness will finally win. What remains to be seen is where each of us personally, now and in the future, will stand in this fight—and how tall we will stand. Will we be true to our last-days, foreordained mission? ("In His Steps," in *1979 Devotional Speeches of the Year* [Provo: Brigham Young University Press, 1980], pp. 59–60.)

The second coming of Jesus will contrast greatly with his first coming. He was born in humble circumstances, but his second appearance will be one of great power and glory. Marvelous signs in heaven will announce it, heavenly hosts will accompany him, and all mankind will witness it together. Yet the world is no more prepared today for his second coming than it was prepared for his birth. The truth of God is obscured by ignorance and sin, and the Church of Jesus Christ, like John of old, is as a voice crying in the wilderness. God needs us as much today as he needed John the Baptist two thousand years ago. The future happiness of thousands and even millions of his children is at stake.

As we fulfill our important responsibilities and share the gospel with others, it is important to follow the example of John and help bring people to the Savior and his atonement. If we are not careful, we may actually come between the Savior and those whom we teach. The Jewish leaders of Jesus' time had changed the laws and administered the church in such a way that the people's worship had been transferred from Jehovah to Jehovah's law. This worship of the law instead of the Lawgiver was just as destructive as idolatry and other forms of false worship because it led the people away from the true and living God.

Whether serving as a parent, a brother or sister, or in a Church calling, our goal should be to help those we serve become spiritually independent and committed to the Savior and his teachings. Elder Henry B. Eyring said, "None of the people for whom you are responsible can be truly served without your bearing testimony, in some way, of the mission of Jesus Christ" ("Come unto Christ," in *Brigham Young University 1989–90 Devotional and Fireside Speeches* [Provo: University Publications, 1990], p. 41).

As parents we sometimes want to answer our children's questions and save them the struggle of getting their answers from the Lord. Our children then become dependent upon us rather than developing a trust in God and in the promptings of his Spirit. It took me many years to realize that the scriptures and the whisperings of the Spirit produce a much greater impact on the hearts of my children than my wise fatherly advice and sincere counsel.

When I started helping them find out what God had said on various subjects and encouraging them to study and ask God what they should do, they began to live the gospel for themselves and for God rather than for me. Like John of old, we need to learn to point those we serve toward Christ. After all, if we are going to be successful parents and teachers, our influence must decrease and the Lord's influence must increase.

Both the negative and positive sides of this important principle are illustrated in the mission field. Some missionaries sincerely but ignorantly teach in such a way that the people become converted to them rather than to Christ and his gospel. The people they are teaching become converted to the missionaries' testimonies and to their love and enthusiasm for the gospel. When the missionaries are transferred, many of these people drift into inactivity. In a very real way, all of us need to be careful that, in our anxiety to help those we love accept and live the gospel, we don't place ourselves between them and our Father in Heaven.

On the positive side, because missionaries are not usually allowed to phone home, they come to rely on their Father in Heaven for guidance and direction. While living at home they may have gone to their parents for advice and counsel, but with this avenue of assistance closed they begin to turn to the Lord for help. What a blessing this is in their lives! This one missionary limitation may lead to the strengthening of thousands of testimonies each year.

One great message that John taught through example was that we can love and develop an influential relationship with those we teach and at the same time direct them to the true nourishment that comes through the Savior and his gospel. Those who were introduced to the gospel by John always loved and appreciated him, but they followed the Savior and partook of the precious blessings that he had to offer.

2

Thou Hast Found Favour with God

LUKE 1:28, 30

When Elisabeth was in her sixth month of pregnancy, the small city of Nazareth became the most important city on earth. Within this city's walls lived the future mother of the Son of God. Mary was espoused to a man named Joseph, which meant that she had made a formal contract of marriage with him that would be finalized in a later ceremony. Even though they did not live together during this betrothal period, it was a much more binding relationship than a modern engagement and could be broken only by a formal divorce. They were considered married by the community and were even referred to as husband and wife.

Since men married as young as sixteen or seventeen years old—almost never older than twenty—and women married as young as fourteen, it's reasonable to assume that Joseph and Mary were still in their teens when the angel Gabriel announced to Mary that she would soon become the mother of the Son of God.

Notice how beautiful and simple the words are that Gabriel used when addressing Mary: "Hail, thou that art highly favoured, the Lord is with thee: blessed art thou among women. . . . Fear not, Mary: for thou hast found favour with God. And, behold, thou shalt conceive in thy womb, and bring forth a son, and shalt call his name Jesus. He shall be great, and shall be called the Son of the Highest." (Luke 1:28–32.)

Mary received no special favors but "found favour" (Luke 1:30) with God the same way that all of us earn his favor: through obedience, both in the pre-earthly existence and here upon the earth. She was "blessed . . . among women" (Luke 1:28) because of her righteousness and her commitment to the Father. There is no doubt that she sought the favor of God more than the favor of men. A careful reading of Luke 1 reveals that she was virtuous, humble, and willing to do whatever the Lord desired of her. Mary is an example of what a woman disciple can and should be.

For Mary to be chosen to carry, bear, and raise the Son of God truly did make her highly favored of the Lord. Yet this description could be used for all women who in some way mother their own or other children here upon the earth. Talking about the special nature of women, Patricia T. Holland said:

> I believe *mother* is one of those very carefully chosen words, one of those rich words—with meaning after meaning after meaning. . . . I believe with all my heart that it is first and foremost a statement about our nature, not a head count of our children.
>
> . . . Some women give birth and raise children but never "mother" them. Others, whom I love with all my heart, "mother" all their lives but have never given birth. And all of us are Eve's daughters, whether we are married or single, maternal or barren. We are created in the image of the Gods to become gods and goddesses. . . . Whatever our circumstance, we can reach out, touch, hold, lift, and nurture. ("'One Thing Needful,'" *Ensign*, October 1987, p. 33.)

As I contemplate the importance of many different women in my own life, I wonder how many women mothered Jesus through his growing-up years and throughout his ministry. As I reflect on the overwhelming importance of my own mother, I come to realize how important Mary and every mother is in God's eternal plan. The humility, love, and strength that so many mothers exhibit are depicted in the following story told by President Thomas S. Monson.

While serving as a mission president, I attended a seminar for all presidents held in Salt Lake City. My wife and I were privileged to devote an evening to meeting the parents of those missionaries who served with us. . . .

Of all the parents whom I met that evening, the best remembered was that mother from Star Valley. As she took my hand in hers I felt the large calluses which revealed the manual labor she daily performed. Almost apologetically, she attempted to excuse her rough hands, her wind-whipped face. She whispered, "Tell our son Spencer that we love him, that we're proud of him, and that we pray daily for him."

Until that night I had never seen an angel nor heard an angel speak. I never again could make that statement, for that angel mother carried with her the Spirit of Christ. She, who with that same hand clasped in the hand of God had walked bravely into the valley of the shadow of death to bring to this mortal life her son, had indelibly impressed my life. ("Profiles of Faith," *Ensign,* November 1978, pp. 56–57.)

Innumerable times every day, the "angel mothers" of this world nurture, encourage, lift, and guide as they quietly and unpretentiously assist God in his sacred work. Just as Mary taught and nurtured the physical Son of God, women throughout the world nurture and teach the spiritual sons and daughters of God. The contribution of these women to the peace and happiness of this world is incalculable.

3

He Shall Be Called the Son of God

LUKE 1:35

When the angel Gabriel told Mary that she was going to bring forth a son, she replied, "How shall this be, seeing I know not a man?"

Gabriel's important and revealing response was, "The Holy Ghost shall come upon thee, and the power of the Highest shall overshadow thee: therefore also that holy thing which shall be born of thee shall be called the Son of God." (Luke 1:34–35.)

Nephi was privileged to see these holy events hundreds of years before they transpired: "I beheld that [Mary] was carried away in the Spirit; and after she had been carried away in the Spirit for the space of a time the angel spake unto me, saying: Look! And I looked and beheld the virgin again, bearing a child in her arms. And the angel said unto me: Behold the Lamb of God, yea, even the Son of the Eternal Father!" (1 Nephi 11:19–21.)

Because of the wording used in the scriptures, especially in Matthew 1:20, some Bible readers have become confused and thought that the Holy Ghost was the father of Jesus. The role the Holy Ghost played in the birth of Jesus was clarified by Elder Bruce R. McConkie: "To be 'carried away in the Spirit' means to be transported bodily from one location to another, as witness the fact that Nephi, at the very time he beheld these visions, had been 'caught away in the Spirit of the Lord' and taken bodily 'into an exceeding high mountain'" (*The Mortal Messiah*, 4 vols. [Salt Lake City: Deseret Book Co., 1979–81], 1:314).

That Jesus is literally the Son of God is of transcending importance. Without this divine Sonship, he could never have become the Savior and Redeemer of the world. Yet much of the Christian world has only a vague, confusing concept concerning Jesus' identity as the Son of God, or accepts him only as a prophet, a successful teacher, or a good man. One common Christian belief is that Jesus was not the literal Son of God any more than all of us are the sons of God. Another tenet is that somehow Jesus is Heavenly Father but is known as Jesus in the flesh; therefore he is not the Son of God but is God himself.

The Atonement is totally dependent on Jesus being the offspring of a mortal mother and an immortal Father. Jesus said: "Therefore doth my Father love me, because I lay down my life, that I might take it again. No man taketh it from me, but I lay it down of myself. I have *power* to lay it down, and I have *power* to take it again." (John 10:17–18; emphasis added.)

Because Jesus had a mortal mother, he was able to suffer physical death. Because he had an immortal Father, he inherited the power to resurrect himself from the dead, which in some way broke the bands of death for all of us.

Emphasizing the importance of this doctrine, Elder McConkie wrote: "The Son of God shall have God as his Father; it is just that simple, and it could not be otherwise. The doctrine of the divine Sonship lies at the foundation of true religion; without it, Christ becomes just another man, a great moral teacher, or what have you, without power to ransom, to redeem, and to save." (*The Mortal Messiah*, 1:314.)

Realizing that Mary was completely overwhelmed and that she had no idea how this holy event was going to take place, the angel used Elisabeth's pregnancy as an example of the power of God, saying, "For with God nothing shall be impossible" (Luke 1:37).

Even though Mary did not understand how these things were going to take place, her humble faith and willing heart led her to say, "Behold the handmaid of the Lord; be it unto me according to thy word" (Luke 1:38). If each member of the Church exhibited a similar attitude, the kingdom of God would roll forth at an unprecedented pace. This is the same attitude Jesus demonstrated in the Garden of Gethsemane when he said, "Not my will, but thine, be done" (Luke 22:42). When we know what the will of God is, the how or why are not all that important. As we start doing what God desires us to do, most of our questions seem to take care of themselves.

In some cases, because of his greater perspective the Lord's desires will differ from our own, but this is not always the case. Many times we underestimate the Lord's willingness to answer our desires and fail to seek some blessing the Lord is willing to give us. Elder Marion G. Romney had an experience that illustrates this point.

In 1967, his beloved wife, Ida, suffered a serious stroke that left her in serious condition. The doctors said that she could be kept alive by artificial means but counseled against it.

As the family tried to prepare themselves for her death, Elder Romney confided to those close to him that in spite of his personal longing for Ida to get well, above all he wanted "the Lord's will to be done and to take what he needed to take without whimpering."

As time went on, Sister Romney's health worsened. Because of an earlier experience, Elder Romney knew that he could never ask the Lord for something that was not in harmony with the Lord's will. Because he wanted to make sure that he had done all that he could do, he fasted and prayed for the ability to show his faith in Ida's behalf yet accept the will of the Lord.

Ida's health continued to fail. One evening, after she had been unable to speak or recognize him, Elder Romney turned to the scriptures, hoping to receive the strength, peace, and guidance that he desperately needed. As he read the following scripture, the Lord touched his heart and he knew that this night this scripture was personal revelation to him.

> Blessed art thou, . . . for those things which thou hast done. . . .
> And thou . . . hast not . . . sought thine own life, but hast sought my will, and to keep my commandments.

And now, because thou hast done this . . . I will bless thee forever; and I will make thee mighty in word and in deed, in faith and in works; yea, even that all things shall be done unto thee according to thy word, for thou shalt not ask that which is contrary to my will. (Helaman 10:4–5.)

For the first time in weeks he felt a tangible peace enter his heart and soul and he knew that his fasting and prayers had been answered. He fell to his knees in thankful prayer. As he concluded with the phrase "Thy will be done," he either felt or heard a voice say, "It is not contrary to my will that Ida be healed."

Even though it was past two o'clock in the morning, he quickly put on his coat and tie and drove to the hospital. There he found his wife still the same. She did not stir as he placed his hands on her head and promised her, with the power of the priesthood, that she would recover completely from her critical illness.

As he concluded the blessing, Ida's eyes opened and, for the first time in months, she spoke to him. She said, "For goodness sakes, Marion, what are you doing here?" Not knowing whether to laugh or cry, he said, "Ida, how are you?" She humorously replied, "Compared to what, Marion? Compared to what?"

From that moment, Sister Romney began to recover, and she lived to see her husband sustained as a member of the First Presidency. (See F. Burton Howard, *Marion G. Romney: His Life and Faith* [Salt Lake City: Bookcraft, 1988], pp. 137–142.)

As we seek the Lord's will in all things, our lives become richer and happier and we come to realize that the Lord is a better judge of what we need than we are. Because he knows what our true needs are (see Matthew 6:8), it is important to learn to counsel with him instead of demand from him. This allows our prayers to become truly effective because we are asking for those things that will be of greatest benefit to us and to those whom we serve. Like Mary we will be able to faithfully say, "Be it unto me according to thy word."

4

The Savior Is Born

LUKE 2:1–20

Were the circumstances surrounding the birth of Jesus left to chance? Was he really born in a stable because there was no room in the inn? Did Bethlehem become his city of birth simply because Caesar Augustus commanded his subjects to register at their cities of ancestry? The answer to these questions is a resounding no! Jesus was born in a stable in Bethlehem because that is where God wanted his Son born. The events surrounding the most important birth in all history were surely carefully guided and orchestrated by our Father in Heaven.

Every twenty years, subjects of the Roman Empire were required to return to their city of ancestry and register for the tax. Bethlehem, the city of ancestry for both Joseph and Mary, was more than eighty dusty miles from where they lived in Nazareth. Since they would walk most if not all of the way, it was at least a three-day trip. Add to this the fact that Mary was "great with child" (Luke 2:5) and we can only imagine the difficulty of the journey.

Mary and Joseph must have known that according to the scriptures the Son of God would be born in Bethlehem. They also knew that the inns would quickly fill because the descendants of David from all over the empire would be returning to Bethlehem. Why, then, didn't they leave earlier so that Jesus could be born in an inn instead of a stable? We can only assume that Mary and Joseph were being directed by the Holy Ghost and that they left Nazareth when the Lord wanted them to.

This leads to the next obvious question: Why would God rather have Jesus born in a stable than an inn? Many have taught that God may have wanted his Son to be born in the most humble of circumstances. Elder Bruce R. McConkie wrote: "Though heaven was his habitation and earth his footstool, he chose to lie as an infant in a manger, surrounded by horses and camels and mules. Though he laid the foundations of the earth, and worlds without number had rolled into orbit at his word, he chose to come into mortality among the beasts of the field. Though he had worn a kingly crown in the eternal courts on high, he chose to breathe as his first mortal breath the stench of a stable." (*The Mortal Messiah,* 4 vols. [Salt Lake City: Deseret Book Co., 1979–81], 1:345.)

Another good reason for not having the Son of God born in an inn is suggested when we realize what the inns were like at the time of Christ. Most of those inns consisted of small cubicles around the outside walls, in which the travelers attempted to sleep. Their animals were tied up in an open court in the middle of the building. There were no front walls to these rooms, so everything that took place in the inn was visible to every other traveler who was camped there. During the census the inns would have been very crowded and noisy, with celebrating and drinking going on late into the night. The unpleasant smell of unwashed bodies, both animal and human, would be stifling, and the filth and litter from uncaring travelers would be everywhere. Even worse than the noise and litter would have been the prostitution that was a common feature at most of the inns.

To have Jesus born in this kind of atmosphere would have been extremely difficult for Mary and Joseph. It also would have made it almost impossible for the shepherds and others who may have visited that night to feel the Spirit and become witnesses of Christ. It is an enormous understatement to say that the inns were not conducive to the Spirit and to what Heavenly Father wanted to accomplish the night Jesus was born.

So, for reasons known to God, Jesus was not born in a house or an inn but was wrapped in "swaddling clothes" and laid in a manger (see Luke 2:7). The custom of that time was to wash newborn babies and rub their skin with salt to toughen their skin. They were then wrapped tightly, with their arms at their sides, in cloth strips four or five inches wide and about five yards long.

The birth of Jesus was not meant to be a secret. Many messengers would be chosen to bear witness of Jesus throughout Israel. The first recorded messengers of his actual birth were the humble shepherds who were abiding in the field with their flocks. Since the flocks reserved for temple sacrifice were kept in the fields near Bethlehem, the chosen shepherds were probably those who were watching and guarding these sheep. These may have been the same sheep that would be sacrificed as a similitude of the future sacrifice Jesus would suffer for all of us. These special shepherds—for special they must have been to be chosen as witnesses—were soon to become sacred witnesses that the Lamb of God, the Savior of the world, had been born.

An angel came to them and proclaimed the long-awaited message of redemption and salvation: "Fear not: for, behold, I bring you good tidings of great joy, which shall be to all people. For unto you is born this day in the city of David a Saviour, which is Christ the Lord." He then gave them a sign so that they could find and recognize the Son of God: they would "find the babe wrapped in swaddling clothes, lying in a manger." (Luke 2:10–12.)

The angel was then joined by "a multitude of the heavenly host praising God, and saying, Glory to God in the highest, and on earth peace, good will toward men" (Luke 2:13–14). Elder Bruce R. McConkie has suggested that a better translation would be, "On earth peace among men of good will" (*Doctrinal New Testament Commentary*, 3 vols. [Salt Lake City: Bookcraft, 1965–73], 1:97). As we contemplate the eternal significance of this great event, it seems reasonable to suppose that we were among the multitude that praised God and shared in the good news of the Savior's birth.

As soon as the angels had left, the shepherds went into Bethlehem to find this baby that would become the Savior of the world. The scriptures state that they "came with haste, and found Mary, and Joseph, and the babe lying in a manger" (Luke 2:16).

We might ask ourselves, Do we hasten to fulfill assignments that we receive from messengers of our Father in Heaven? Do we hasten to come to Christ and become a witness of his saving truths?

The shepherds were not called to be merely spectators but to be witnesses that the promised Messiah had been born. They "made known abroad" (Luke 2:17) the things which they had seen and heard. If you had been one of the people in Bethlehem whom the shepherds told, what would you have done? I think I would have quickly gone to the stable myself so that I could participate in this joyous birth. It would not be surprising to someday find out that many people visited the holy stable that night.

Messengers are still being sent forth to testify of the Son of God. It is not necessary to have seen the Savior in order to testify of him, for the Holy Ghost will bear witness of him to all those who sincerely seek him. Just as the shepherds did two thousand years ago, we too can "make known abroad" the good news concerning Jesus and his gospel. Through bearing our testimonies with the power and guidance of the Spirit, we can assist in spreading the saving knowledge of his birth, teachings, and atonement.

5

The Sermon on the Mount: Attitudes That Bring Divine Happiness

MATTHEW 5–7; 3 NEPHI 12–14

A few summers ago, Elder Jack H Goaslind followed a car on the freeway that presented an interesting picture. As you read his colorful description, you may notice some similarities between the family he observed and trips your own family has taken. "It was a large station wagon that had obviously endured many road skirmishes. The top rack was loaded with luggage; the seats were loaded with people. Four bare feet hung out the rear window, and elbows and arms hung out the side windows. In the front seat, the mother was wrestling with a feisty child while simultaneously trying to calm an upset infant. The father was desperately trying to negotiate the heavy traffic. It was obviously vacation time for this family. As I surveyed the situation with some degree of empathy, I noticed a bumper sticker which read, 'Are we having fun yet?'"

Elder Goaslind went on to suggest that this story "reveals a very real aspect of the human condition: the largely unfulfilled pursuit of happiness." ("Happiness," *Ensign,* May 1986, p. 52.)

The number-one pursuit of most people throughout the world is the search for happiness, yet many if not most find that happiness continues to elude them. The quest for happiness usually takes the form of investing great amounts of time and money into a variety of forms of amusement and recreation. For instance, in 1985 Americans spent $700 million a day—or more than $8,000 each second—on entertainment and recreation. During an average day that same year, Americans purchased 50,000 new television sets, paid out $14.3 million for lottery tickets, ate 5.8 million pounds of chocolate candy, and watched 1.5 billion hours of television. (See "What a Difference an Average Day Makes," *Deseret News,* 4 July 1985.)

Even more serious than seeking lasting happiness through entertainment is the false assumption that happiness can be gained through sin. This same survey found that during an average day in 1985 Americans drank 15.7 million gallons of beer and spent over $40 million on prostitutes and that 5,000 people tried cocaine for the first time (ibid.). The primary motive behind these and most other sins seems to be the desire for happiness. Many yield to temptation because it seems to offer a shortcut to happiness—a chance to enjoy pleasure without putting forth much effort. The happiness that some foolishly seek through sin is nothing but a mirage, for wickedness never has and never will bring happiness.

Only those who come to realize that the source of happiness is not found around them but within themselves find true and lasting happiness. One of the best discussions of the difference between momentary pleasure and lasting happiness was presented by Elder James E. Talmage. As you read his insightful words, notice the role Satan plays as he counterfeits the true happiness all of us are seeking.

> The present is an age of pleasure-seeking, and men are losing their sanity in the mad rush for sensations that do but excite and disappoint. In this day of counterfeits, adulterations, and base imitations, the devil is busier than he has ever been in the course of human history, in the manufacture of pleasures, both old and new; and these he offers for sale in most attractive fashion, falsely labeled, *Happiness.* In this soul-destroying craft he is without a peer; he has had centuries of experience and practice, and by his skill he controls

the market. He has learned the tricks of the trade, and knows well how to catch the eye and arouse the desire of his customers. He puts up the stuff in bright-colored packages, tied with tinsel string and tassel; and crowds flock to his bargain counters, hustling and crushing one another in their frenzy to buy.

Follow one of the purchasers as he goes off gloatingly with his gaudy packet, and watch him as he opens it. . . . He has expected fragrant happiness, but uncovers only an inferior brand of pleasure, the stench of which is nauseating.

Elder Talmage goes on to explain that "happiness leaves no bad after-taste, it is followed by no depressing reaction; it calls for no repentance, brings no regret, entails no remorse; pleasure too often makes necessary repentance, contrition, and suffering; and, if indulged to the extreme, it brings degradation and destruction." (Quoted in *Jesus the Christ* [Salt Lake City: Deseret Book Co., 1973], pp. 247–48.)

Joseph Smith said that "happiness is the object and design of our existence; and will be the end thereof, if we pursue the path that leads to it." He also taught the following concepts that clearly reveal the path to happiness and joy.

1. "This path is virtue, uprightness, faithfulness, holiness, and keeping all the commandments of God."
2. "In obedience there is joy and peace unspotted."
3. God never "will institute an ordinance or give a commandment to His people that is not calculated in its nature to promote that happiness which He has designed." (See *Teachings of the Prophet Joseph Smith*, comp. Joseph Fielding Smith [Salt Lake City: Deseret Book Co., 1977], pp. 255–57.)

Many feel that the commandments of God are meant to take away our freedom or limit our happiness. This could not be further from the truth. The principles of the gospel are literally the guidelines that help us find true happiness and joy. One of the first steps in our quest for happiness is to realize that the gospel plan is *the* plan of happiness. Sometimes we don't enjoy the happiness that could be ours simply because we haven't made the commitment of obedience necessary to receive this great blessing. Referring to the importance of this commitment, Elder Jack H Goaslind said: "You cannot succeed with sporadic little flashes of effort. Constant and valiant living is necessary. . . . It requires that you make a deliberate decision to do good and then carry out your decision. Do it. Simply do it, and do it long enough that you experience success, no matter how hard it may seem. Your victory over self brings communion with God and results in happiness— lasting and eternal happiness." ("Happiness," *Ensign,* May 1986, pp. 53–54.)

As Elder Goaslind suggests, happiness does not come from outward obedience alone but from the changing of our attitudes and motives—the growth toward godhood that takes place when we obey for the right reasons. The closer our desires, attitudes, and actions approach those of the Savior and of our Father in Heaven, the more joyful and blessed our lives will become.

An exceptional source to turn to in identifying attitudes and behaviors that bring happiness is the Sermon on the Mount. In this simple but profound sermon, Jesus teaches us the attitudes we can develop and the things we can do to gain the happiness that he and our Father in Heaven enjoy.

The Savior sets the tone of the sermon by using the word *blessed* nine times in the first eleven verses (see Matthew 5:1–11). In the Greek text, the word *blessed* is *makarios,* which refers to a state of divine happiness (see Catherine Thomas, "'Blessed Are Ye . . . ,'" *Ensign,* June 1987, p. 6). The happiness we often think of is dependent on outward circumstances, but divine happiness refers to the well-being and spiritual joy of those who share in the blessings of the kingdom of God. In the Sermon on the Mount, Jesus tells us how to find divine happiness in this life and a fulness of joy in the life to come. Each time the word *blessed* is used, it would be helpful to substitute the word *happy* in its place. Thus, "Blessed are the merciful" would read, "Happy are the merciful" (see Matthew 5:7).

Jesus made it clear that Church membership and obedience to the prophets and Apostles are absolutely necessary in our search for true happiness. He stretched forth his hands to the Nephite multitude and said:

> Blessed [happy] are ye if ye shall give heed unto the words of these twelve whom I have chosen from among you to minister unto you, and to be your servants; and unto them I have given power that they may baptize you with water; and after that ye are baptized with water, behold, I will baptize you with fire and with the Holy Ghost; therefore blessed [happy] are ye if ye shall believe in me and be baptized, after that ye have seen me and know that I am.
>
> . . . Yea, blessed [happy] are they who shall believe in your words, and come down into the depths of humility and be baptized, for they shall be visited with fire and with the Holy Ghost, and shall receive a remission of their sins. (3 Nephi 12:1–2.)

Our understanding of the true source of happiness is greatly expanded when we realize that repentance, baptism, and receiving the Holy Ghost are prerequisites to receiving the joy, peace, and happiness that we desire. In order to develop the attitudes and behavior that bring this happiness, we need the strength and guidance that the Holy Ghost can give us. Membership in God's church also gives us a better opportunity to understand the Atonement. This understanding can bring comfort, perspective, and peace in times of trial and distress. Therefore, happiness does not come to the poor in spirit but to those poor in spirit who come unto Christ (see 3 Nephi 12:3.)

On Judgment Day, what we have done will undoubtedly not be as important as what kind of person we have become. Most likely, the question won't be whether or not we have attended church or paid our tithing. The question will be, Have we developed celestial attributes so we will feel comfortable in the presence of God? Thoughts and desires as well as actions are extremely important in shaping our celestial attitudes and character. This is why genuine growth and happiness come from within. One writer explains it this way:

The storms of life will surely create tumult and beat upon us, but the Savior's message in the Sermon on the Mount is that the basis of real happiness does not lie in trying to subdue the storms outside us, but in sacrificing our sins and allowing the Savior to activate righteousness within us.

Indeed, without the storms we might have thought happiness lay in our own ability to control people and events to our own specifications. Instead, the storms propel us to God, where we may "receive revelation upon revelation, knowledge upon knowledge," so that we may "know the mysteries and peaceable things—that which bringeth joy, that which bringeth life eternal." (D&C 42:61.) (Thomas, "'Blessed Are Ye . . . ,'" p. 9.)

In the Sermon on the Mount, the Savior outlined many of the attitudes that lead to happiness and, eventually, joy and eternal life. For example, he taught that humility, meekness, and a forgiving nature lead to greater happiness than do their opposites of pride, arrogance, resentment, and bitterness. He taught that peace and joy come from controlling our thoughts, not just our actions. He emphasized that when we pray and give service, our motives determine whether or not God answers and blesses us. He counseled us to avoid unrighteous judgment and encouraged us to treat others as we would like to be treated.

Some of these teachings will be discussed in future chapters, but it would be beneficial to all of us to carefully study the Sermon on the Mount. Each teaching in this great sermon suggests an attitude that, if developed, will bring us more happiness and joy. By studying, pondering, and committing ourselves to the development of these attitudes, we become more like the Savior and invite into our lives the peace and happiness that only the Spirit can bring.

6

Blessed Are the Poor in Spirit . . . Who Come unto Me

MATTHEW 5:3; 3 NEPHI 12:3

The story is told of a battleship assigned to a training squadron. It had been at sea on maneuvers in heavy weather for several days. As night fell visibility was poor because of patchy fog, so the captain remained on the bridge.

Shortly after dark, the lookout on the wing of the bridge reported a light on the starboard bow. When the captain asked if the light was steady or moving astern, he was informed that it was steady. This was serious because it indicated his ship was on a dangerous collision course with another ship.

The captain quickly gave the order to signal the other ship that it was on a collision course and to advise it to change its course twenty degrees. Back came a signal advising the first ship to change its course twenty degrees.

This upset the captain, so he ordered a signal sent telling the other ship that he was a captain and again ordering it to change its course twenty degrees. The signaled reply was, "I'm a seaman second class, and you had better change course twenty degrees."

By now the captain was furious. He sent a message stating that his ship was a battleship and that the other ship better change its course twenty degrees. Back came the flashing light, "I'm a lighthouse." The captain's arrogance was quickly replaced with concern, and he immediately changed the course of his ship.

Heavenly Father and his son Jesus Christ are our lighthouse in a world of darkness and danger. If we are willing to respond to his light and chart a safe course, the Lord will guide us through the perils and hazards that constantly confront us. The willingness to accept guidance from our Father in Heaven and his servants here upon the earth is referred to in the scriptures as having a broken heart and a contrite spirit. This quality or attitude of humility is absolutely essential in our quest for happiness. Humility is the very foundation of obedience to the principles and teachings of God, which if followed will bring divine happiness into our lives.

Jesus said, "Yea, blessed are the poor in spirit who come unto me, for theirs is the kingdom of heaven" (3 Nephi 12:3). To be poor in spirit is to be humble and teachable. It is the opposite of pride, conceit, and self-righteousness. Humility is the attitude we feel as we come to realize the great difference between us and God and begin to truly discern how much we need his guidance and help. This difference is illustrated in the following story by S. Michael Wilcox.

> One Christmas, my Cub Scout son needed two dollars to make me a present. On Christmas morning, he was so excited about it that in spite of the many brightly wrapped packages with his name on them, he insisted I open his present first. It was a pencil holder for my office—made from a jar covered with brightly colored macaroni. The two dollars bought pencils and erasers. I was pleased with his innocence and love. He then eagerly turned to his own presents.
>
> In comparison with the bounteous gifts the Father bestows upon us—life, the Atonement, the gospel, prophets, scriptures, temples— our gifts to him are like jars covered with macaroni. It's the best we can do, and he accepts our efforts with pleasure. The realization of the difference between us and Him produces deep humility and blessedness. ("The Beatitudes—Pathway to the Savior," *Ensign,* January 1991, p. 20.)

An unhappy contrast to this important perspective was displayed in the life of Sidney Rigdon. Sacred Book of Mormon scripture tells us that Jesus would "suffer temptations, and pain of body, hunger, thirst, and fatigue, even more than man can suffer, except it be unto death" (Mosiah 3:7). Yet when Brother Rigdon was released from Liberty Jail he said that "the sufferings of Jesus Christ were a fool to his" (*History of the Church* 3:264).

When Sidney allowed arrogance and pride to replace his humility, he lost his realization of his deep need for God and began a downward slide that left him a bitter man. His conceit and pride led to the loss of his faith, his priesthood, and all the happiness and joy that could have been his.

Compare Sidney Rigdon's arrogant and self-centered attitude to the attitude of the humble priesthood leader described in the following story by Elder Henry B. Eyring:

> When I was the president of Ricks College years ago, I remember having a man who was my priesthood leader come to my house each month to interview me about my home teaching. He brought with him a gray notebook in which he wrote notes. He recorded not only my report as a home teacher, but my observations about the gospel and life as well.
>
> I remember at first being very flattered. Then one Sunday he and I were visiting what was then called junior Sunday School. He was a few rows in front of me. The speaker was a little girl, no more than six or seven, probably not yet old enough to have the gift of the Holy Ghost. I glanced over at the man and noticed with surprise that he had that same gray notebook open. As the little girl spoke, he was writing with as much speed and intensity as he had in the study of my home. ("Listen Together," *Brigham Young University 1988–89 Devotional and Fireside Speeches* [Provo: Brigham Young University Press, 1989], p. 13.)

Because of this man's humility and faith, he felt that God could speak to him as clearly through this young child as through President Eyring, and he learned from the things she had to say.

Because of our basic nature, it seems that humility is difficult to obtain and even more difficult to retain. If we are not careful, we may even begin to feel proud about our great humility. When someone asked President Spencer W. Kimball how he kept humble, he replied, "Sometimes I am humble and sometimes I am un-humble." He then gave a formula for developing humility that he felt would never fail. I have taken the liberty to group his formula into the following steps:

1. "First, you evaluate yourself. What am I? I am the circle. I am the hole in the doughnut. I would be nothing without the Lord. My breath, my brains, my hearing, my sight, my locomotion, my everything depends upon the Lord."

2. "Then we pray, and pray often, and we will not get up from our knees until we have communicated. The line may be down; we may have let it fall to pieces, but I will not get up from my knees until I have established communication—if it is twenty minutes, if it is all night like Enos. . . . If it takes all day long, you stay on your knees until your unhumbleness has dissipated, until you feel the humble spirit and realize, 'I could die this minute if it were not for the Lord's good grace. I am dependent upon him—totally dependent upon him.'"

3. "Then you read the scriptures. Could you read these scriptures . . . and not be lifted and inspired? Can you read about the prophets—David O. McKay—and not feel weak and small in comparison? . . . And when you have success, you do not glory in it for you, you glory in it for the Lord." (*The Teachings of Spencer W. Kimball* [Salt Lake City: Bookcraft, 1982], pp. 233–34.)

As we become more humble, we become more obedient, which allows us to enjoy the blessings of the spirit in greater abundance. We find ourselves accepting counsel and chastisement more easily. We begin to forgive those who have offended us and desire to render more selfless service. We seem to submit more to the will of God, and we work harder at putting him first in our lives. All these things lead to greater happiness and joy because our lives are more in tune with those things that bring these great blessings.

Just as most sins seem to stem from feelings of pride (see Ezra Taft Benson, "Beware of Pride," *Ensign,* May 1989, pp. 4–7), obedience and righteousness seem to flow from deep feelings of humility and submissiveness to God. Jesus may very well have placed humility as the first Beatitude because it is the foundation of all the other virtues and blessings. It is the very beginning of our journey toward peace, eternal life, and a fullness of joy.

7

"Yea, Yea" or "Nay, Nay"

MATTHEW 5:33–37

While I was growing up, my father taught me over and over again that a person's word was his or her bond. To me this meant that once we give our word, we should do our very best to keep it even if it becomes difficult to do so. Recently I mentioned the phrase "Our word is our bond" to my seminary students, and not one of them had any idea what this meant. It seemed that I was plowing new ground with many of my students as we discussed the meaning of the phrase. This is not surprising, because the world seems very confused when it comes to applying or even understanding basic principles of honesty and integrity.

When it was revealed that a prominent political figure was cheating on his wife, he said that his actions were irrelevant because he was a man of high moral values—a man of honesty and integrity. As a panel of leading news people discussed the politician's immoral behavior, they arrived at the same conclusion. They felt that his private life should have no bearing on the way he fulfilled his public responsibility. None of the reporters admitted any correlation between cheating on his wife and lacking honesty and integrity. They failed to consider the fact that he was breaking some of the most sacred and personal promises he had ever made—those he had made with his wife the day they were married. Somehow, to both him and the news people, he could be dishonest and disloyal to his wife yet still be filled with integrity.

The realm of professional athletics presents numerous examples of this spiritual and intellectual blindness when it comes to keeping one's word. On a regular basis we read about athletes with multimillion-dollar contracts who threaten to refuse to play if their contracts are not renegotiated. They consider this good business practice rather than a breach of their word.

Lack of commitment to one's word is not confined to politics and sports but can be found in most areas of our society. Such an attitude is accompanied by contention, distrust, unhappiness, and the loss of the Spirit. Because of the prevalence of this problem and because of the importance of personal integrity in our quest for peace and happiness, the Savior addressed this crucial issue in the Sermon on the Mount. Comparing his higher law to the prepatory law of Moses, he said: "Ye have heard that it hath been said by them of old time, Thou shalt not forswear thyself, but shalt perform unto the Lord thine oaths: but I say unto you, Swear not at all. . . . But let your communication be, Yea, yea; Nay, nay: for whatsoever is more than these cometh of evil." (Matthew 5:33–34, 37.)

In previous dispensations, the taking of oaths was a regular part of people's lives. They would swear in the name of God or on their own heads or on some other sacred thing that they would keep their word. When oaths were sworn by people who valued their word above their lives, others relied on these oaths with absolute confidence. The law of Moses stated, "If a man vow a vow unto the Lord, or swear an oath to bind his soul with a bond; he shall not break his word, he shall do according to all that proceedeth out of his mouth" (Numbers 30:2). To "forswear thyself" meant to break your oath or perjure yourself.

The Book of Mormon illustrates the importance early-day Saints placed on promises that were accompanied with an oath. When Nephi killed Laban and took the brass plates, Laban's servant Zoram accompanied him out of the city. Nephi faced a problem: if Zoram was allowed to go free, he would tell the city leaders what had taken place and the Jews would follow Nephi and his family into the wilderness. Nephi swore an oath that he would spare Zoram's life if Zoram would go with them and become one of them. Zoram responded by making an oath that he would tarry with them from that time forth. The confidence that accompanied these oaths is clearly illustrated when Nephi states, "When Zoram had made an oath unto us, our fears did cease concerning him" (1 Nephi 4:37).

Sometimes those who lie fail to realize the spirit they are responding to and the effect it has on their spiritual growth and happiness. Elder Mark E. Petersen discusses the seriousness of lying and identifies the source of all lies in the following quote:

> But in our society, is there anything more widespread than the tendency to lie and deceive?
>
> It is the lie of the drug peddler that tempts a child to indulge, and the lie of the seducer that persuades a girl to surrender her virtue.
>
> It is the lie of the shyster that traps his victim in a fraudulent deal.
>
> It is the lie of the tax evader that puts him behind bars, and the lie of the student that turns him into a cheat at school.
>
> It is the lie of the child—and too often also of the parent—that creates the generation gap.
>
> It is the lie of the shoddy workman that hides a faulty repair.
>
> It is living lie upon lie that makes a man a hypocrite. . . .
>
> It is the desire to lie and cheat which turns a mother into a shoplifter and the child who assists her into a potential criminal.
>
> It is the lie on the lips of the neighborhood gossip that brings character assassination to many innocent victims. . . .
>
> We Latter-day Saints believe in God and because we believe in him we also believe there is a devil.
>
> But the devil himself is a liar—the father of lies, and those who choose to cheat and lie and deceive and misrepresent become his slaves. (*The Way of the Master* [Salt Lake City: Bookcraft, 1974], pp. 166–68.)

Sometimes, if we are not very careful, we fail to keep our word and yet we still consider ourselves honest and upright citizens of the Lord's kingdom. How many priesthood brethren have said that they would be home teachers but fail month after month to contact some or all their families? How many sisters have made the same pledge about visiting teaching but only keep their word if it is convenient? How many church positions are only half-heartedly performed even though pledges of service have been given? How many temple or service assignments are accepted each week that go unfulfilled?

When Jesus said that our communication should be "Yea, yea" or "Nay, nay," he was ruling out vocal or internal responses such as "Maybe," "Probably," "If I get the time," or "If something doesn't come up." He wants us to say yes and then strive to keep our word at all costs. If we are not going to seriously endeavor to keep our word, he would rather have us say no so that someone else can be assigned to do the work that needs to be done.

This quality of total honesty should be so much a part of us that it permeates all our actions and conversations wherever we might be. For example, let's suppose we are selling a car and some-one offers us a thousand dollars. We accept their offer, but, before we can sign any papers, another person offers us eleven hundred dollars. The world's honesty would have us sell the car to the second buyer because no papers have been signed, but Jesus said that our word needs no notarized contracts or promissory notes—no witnesses or oaths—in order for it to be binding upon us. We would sell the car for a thousand dollars to the first buyer because we had said yes to the offer. We would keep our word.

In a letter to a friend, Abraham Lincoln described an experi-ence that demonstrates the kind of commitment the Savior taught. A married lady he knew said that she was going to visit her sister. She said that she would bring her sister back with her if Lincoln would commit to marry the sister. He had seen the sister three years before and, he wrote, "thought her intelligent and agreeable, and saw no good objection to plodding life through hand in hand with her"; so he agreed to marry her.

Time passed, and the lady returned with her sister. The prob-lem was that the sister looked nothing like Lincoln remembered, and, to say it kindly, he found her less than appealing. After describing her and sharing his own disappointment, Lincoln wrote the following:

I was not . . . pleased with her. But what could I do? I had told her sister I would take her for better or for worse; and I made a point of honor and conscience in all things to stick to my word, especially if others had been induced to act on it, which in this case I had no doubt they had; for I was now fairly convinced that no other man on earth would have her. . . . "Well," thought I, "I have said it, and, be the consequences what they may, it shall not be my fault if I fail to do it." At once I determined to consider her my wife; and, this done, all my powers of discovery were put to work in search of perfections in her which might be fairly set off against her defects. . . .

. . . After I had delayed the matter as long as I thought I could in honor do . . . , I concluded I might as well bring it to a consummation without further delay; and so I mustered my resolution, and made the proposal to her direct; but, shocking to relate, she answered, No. At first I supposed she did it through . . . modesty . . . ; but on my renewal of the charge, I found she repelled it with greater firmness than before. I tried it again and again, . . . with the same want of success.

I finally was forced to give it up; at which I very unexpectedly found myself mortified almost beyond endurance. . . . My vanity was deeply wounded by the reflection . . . that she, whom I had taught myself to believe nobody else would have, had actually rejected me with all my fancied greatness. (Quoted in Carl Sandburg, *Abraham Lincoln: The Prairie Years,* 2 vols. [New York: Harcourt, Brace and Co., 1926], 1:227, 228–29.)

We came here to become like God so that we can eventually enjoy the fulness of joy that is his. God does "not walk in crooked paths; neither doth he vary from that which he hath said" (Alma 7:20). As we learn to keep our word and not vary from what we say, we develop an important attribute of godhood. No matter how negative the consequences might be of keeping our word, they are minute in importance compared to the blessings that come from the practice of honesty and integrity in our lives. What earthly consequence could outweigh having the Holy Ghost to guide us in this life and enjoying the peace and joy of eternal life in the world to come?

8

The Second Mile

MATTHEW 5:41

While serving as a missionary couple in England, Don and Marian Summers were asked to serve their last six months in the Swindon Branch. Swindon had been a branch for eighty years, but just a few members of the branch were active.

The Summerses' first sabbath in the branch was somewhat disheartening. They met in a cold, rented hall, and only seventeen members were present, including the president of the mission, his wife, and four missionaries. Still wearing their winter coats, everyone huddled around a small heater while they listened to the Sunday School lesson.

Instead of becoming discouraged or giving up, Elder and Sister Summers rolled up their sleeves and went into action. They were told by one of the members that they should never mention tithing in the branch because the members did not believe in tithing and it would just upset them. However, they disregarded this counsel and taught the principle of tithing along with all the other wonderful principles of the gospel. They visited the home of every member of the branch, and the hearts of many were softened. As they and the branch president worked tirelessly, faith and activity started to increase.

Many firesides were held, and the couple began to work closely with the stake and full-time missionaries. They promised the Lord that they would not let one new or activated member fall by the wayside while they were still in Swindon. In the following excerpt from one of their letters, they share an experience they enjoyed while striving to keep this promise:

> One young couple had a difficult adjustment to make as their customs, manners, and dress were different. They became offended at suggestions for changes. The couple twice wrote to the bishop [since by then it was a ward] and asked to have their names removed from the Church records. In the last letter they forbade any of the members to visit them, so Marian and I went to the florist and purchased a beautiful plant of chrysanthemums and had it delivered to the young couple. It was a simple note: "*We love you; we miss you; we need you. Please come back.*" Signed, Swindon Ward.
>
> The next Sunday was fast and testimony meeting and our last Sunday in Swindon. There were 103 members in attendance compared to seventeen six months before. The young couple was there and, in bearing his testimony, the husband thanked the Swindon Ward for not giving up on them. (Quoted in Robert D. Hales, "'Some Have Compassion, Making a Difference,'" *Ensign,* May 1987, p. 77.)

The same attitude that brought happiness and success to Elder and Sister Summers brought great joy to a ward in Salt Lake City. When Thomas S. Monson was the bishop of the ward, he learned that a Latter-day Saint family from Germany would be moving into the area within a few weeks. After being shown the run-down apartment the family was going to occupy, Bishop Monson was concerned and mentioned the situation in a ward welfare committee meeting. Before long, the leaders of each organization—the high priests, the seventies, the elders, the Relief Society—had volunteered to perform specific tasks in an effort to renovate the apartment.

When the family arrived from Germany, they went to the apartment and were met there by ward members who had gathered to greet them. In the apartment there was new paint, new wallpaper, new carpet, new electrical wiring, new appliances, and an ample supply of food. The group sang Christmas hymns together. President Monson describes what happened next:

At the conclusion, the father, realizing that all of this was his, took me by the hand to express his thanks. His emotion was too great. He buried his head in my shoulder and repeated the words, "Mein Bruder, mein Bruder, mein Bruder."

As we walked down the stairs and out into the night air, it was snowing. Not a word was spoken. Then a young girl asked, "Bishop, I feel better inside than I have ever felt before. Can you tell me why?" (Thomas S. Monson, "The Bishop—Center Stage in Welfare," *Ensign*, November 1980, p. 91.)

In both of these stories, Church members went above and beyond the normal fulfillment of their responsibilities and received great happiness and joy in return. This idea of doing more than is required is sometimes referred to as going the extra mile or going the second mile. A common phrase that many of us may have heard is that most of the blessings are found in the second mile. The origin of these ideas may have been a custom that was practiced in Jesus' day, a custom that he referred to in the Sermon on the Mount. This teaching is just one sentence long, but understanding and following this principle may have a tremendous impact on our personal growth and happiness as well as on the growth of the whole Church. Jesus said, "And whosoever shall compel thee to go a mile, go with him twain" (Matthew 5:41).

Apparently Jesus was referring to the Roman law that authorized troops passing through to compel local people to carry their belongings. The Greek verb translated as *compel* in the King James Version of the Bible comes from a Persian word that means "to press into service." The same verb is used in Matthew 27:32, where the Roman soldiers press Simon into service to carry Jesus' cross. This practice caused great inconvenience to those who were pressed into service. Not only did they have to carry the equipment of their captors but they had to put off their personal needs and desires until a future time. Since the Jews already hated the Romans, being pressed into service by Roman soldiers just made things worse.

The disciples of Christ have been given the responsibility of taking the gospel to all the world. This cannot happen as long as we consider others our enemies and are considered enemies by them. Consider how the relationship between a soldier and a Christian Jew would have changed if the counsel of Jesus was followed. Service rendered during the first mile was given out of force and necessity, but the second mile was voluntarily given out of love and a desire to help. With this in mind, what would have happened if someone pressed into service said to the soldier: "I have really come to enjoy your company during this time that we have spent together. I would like to carry your belongings another mile or two so we can get better acquainted"? Their relationship would probably have immediately changed for the better. Respect, a better understanding, and even friendship may very well have replaced distrust and hatred. These positive changes would take place because of the very nature of the second mile—the mile that is not given out of duty but out of love.

The brother from Germany wasn't touched as much by the apartment as by the love the apartment represented. The young couple in Swindon came back because they realized that the people in the ward truly cared for them.

The motivation of home teachers who visit on the last day of the month, try to contact their families only once, or give little thought to their visits is generally one of duty. Because the families they visit usually realize what home teaching duties are, this minimum service seldom brings about a change of heart. Families begin to respond when their home teachers go the second mile and give extra service that is not required. They respond because they realize their home teachers really do care about them. This extra service not only benefits the families but blesses the home teachers as well. Love, peace, and joy increase in their hearts.

As we think about people who have made a real difference in our lives, chances are they have shown their love for us in many extra ways. As I ponder my growing-up years, four people come to mind. I know that each of these people truly cared for me by the way they fulfilled their church callings. Even as a youngster growing up, I knew that they were giving much more than was required, and I responded to their gifts of time and love. They may not realize the effect they have had on my life, but I will forever be grateful that they were not afraid to travel the extra mile in my behalf. I have no idea how many other young people have been affected by their willing service, but I'm sure there are many.

Sometimes just one act of going beyond what is required and expected may affect thousands of souls. Such was the case with Yupha Thubthimthong, a young Church member in Thailand. A passenger train had collided head-on with a cargo train, and many people had been killed or severely injured. A service group that Yupha belonged to had been asked to help in the gruesome task of pulling bodies from the wreckage and readying the injured for transportation to the hospital. With strength she received from the Spirit, Yupha was doing her best to help the injured when she was attacked by a woman brandishing a stick. The woman screamed at her: "My children are dead because of you! Look at the destruction your carelessness and negligence have caused!" The woman had lost two of her children in the wreck and, consumed with grief, had mistaken Yupha for a railroad employee.

As Yupha tried to explain that she was not a railroad employee but was only trying to help, three police officers came to her assistance. When they indicated they might arrest the mother, Yupha quickly came to her aid and asked them not to. The police were surprised and protested that the woman had tried to hit her, but Yupha said: "I'm not afraid. Heavenly Father teaches that we are all brothers and sisters. We must love one another. She will not harm me."

The police reluctantly released the woman, and Yupha returned to her dreadful task. Several hours later Yupha responded to a desperate call for type O blood. A small girl was about to undergo lifesaving surgery, and the hospital's blood supply had been depleted. Because her blood was badly need, much more than the usual pint was drawn out of Yupha's veins.

Not realizing that she should rest, she immediately left the hospital and returned to the accident scene. By late afternoon the worst chores had been completed, and Yupha prepared to leave for home so she could take care of her own family. Before she could go, she and the other volunteers were asked to meet at the hospital so that the director could thank them personally.

The Minister of Public Health was also there, and he offered his gratitude for the willing service they had rendered. About this time, the grief-stricken mother who had attacked Yupha entered the room. She was searching for someone, and the doctor accompanying her asked if there was a Yupha in the group. Before Yupha could identify herself, the woman spotted her in the crowd and quickly ran to her. As the woman embraced her and burst into tears, Yupha looked toward the doctor for some explanation. The doctor explained that her donation of blood had saved the life of the woman's daughter, and she had come to thank her.

After expressing her gratitude to Yupha, the woman asked her how she had been able to stay so calm and serene when she had been so angry at her. Yupha explained again that the Church had taught her that all of us are brothers and sisters and that we should love everyone no matter who they are or what they have done.

Dr. Martin, the Minister of Public Health, saw and heard this exchange between Yupha and the grateful mother. He had previously been head of the Department of Education, which supervised the Department of Religion. This department had imposed visa restrictions on the Latter-day Saint missionaries. After seeing the way in which Yupha reacted in a difficult situation, Dr. Martin recognized the value of Latter-day Saint missionary work. Meanwhile the mother requested information about Yupha's church and asked if it would be permissible for her to attend. Yupha assured her that she would always be welcome. (See Carole Osborne Cole, "Train Wreck!" *Ensign,* January 1981, pp. 56–57.)

Although Yupha's attitude of love and forgiveness went far beyond what the world expects, she simply reacted the way all true followers of the Savior would respond under similar circumstances. The Lord expects more from us than the world does.

Along with Yupha, all of us committed to the extra mile of service when we were baptized. We promised to love God with all our might, mind, and strength and to love our neighbor as ourselves. As we do this, we will find our lives filled with meaning and happiness because people really do respond to those who make a habit of traveling the second mile. Like the young woman in President Monson's ward, we will find ourselves saying, "I feel better inside than I have ever felt before."

9

Forgive Us Our Debts, as We Forgive Our Debtors

MATTHEW 6:12–15

Many years ago Brother Frederick Babbel accompanied Elder Ezra Taft Benson as he toured the British mission. After speaking in one of the meetings, Brother Babbel was asked to administer to two members who were present. The first blessing was given to a sister in her seventh month of pregnancy who was having serious complications. Both she and her husband were afraid that she might lose the baby. As he proceeded with the blessing, Brother Babbel felt a tremendous surge of power, and the expectant mother was immediately healed.

The second person who needed a blessing was a three-year-old boy from Scotland who had been a deaf-mute since birth. His parents had traveled to London so that he might receive a special blessing. As Brother Babbel placed his hands on the young boy's head, he felt the power of the Lord and knew that the young boy could be healed instantly.

However, before he could say a word, the Spirit told him that the boy would be healed that very night if his parents would lose the hatred they had in their hearts. This troubled Brother Babbel a great deal because he did not want to question the attitudes of the parents, but the Spirit restrained him from sealing the anointing and giving the boy a blessing.

After pausing for a moment, he removed his hands from the

boy's head and asked the parents, "What is it that you hate so deeply?"

They were startled and surprised, and the husband finally said, "We can't tell you."

Brother Babbel replied that he didn't need to know but that, as he had placed his hands on their son's head, the Spirit had assured him that the boy would be healed that very night and restored to them whole if they would only lose the hatred they carried in their hearts.

After several troubled glances between the husband and the wife, the husband said, "Well, if that is the case, our son will have to go through life as he is, because we won't give up our hating." Brother Babbel concluded this experience by saying, "I felt that I had been prevented from pronouncing a blessing that might have resulted in the salvation of the entire family." (See Frederick W. Babbel, *On Wings of Faith* [Salt Lake City: Bookcraft, 1972], pp. 160–61.)

This couple's refusal to forgive affected much more than their son's physical condition. By clinging to their hate, they continued to inflict great spiritual and emotional damage to themselves. In fact, if they do not come to the point where they can freely forgive and purge the hate from their hearts, they will never enjoy peace and happiness during this life or experience the joy that accompanies eternal life.

In the scripture referred to as the Lord's Prayer, the Savior taught that we should ask God to "forgive us our debts [offenses, faults, sins], as we forgive our debtors" (Matthew 6:12). He went on to explain, "If ye forgive men their trespasses, your heavenly Father will also forgive you: But if ye forgive not men their trespasses, neither will your Father forgive your trespasses" (Matthew 6:14–15).

Referring to these verses, Elder James E. Talmage wrote: "He who can thus pray with full intent and unmixed purpose merits forgiveness. In this specification of personal supplication we are taught to expect only as we deserve. . . . Forgiveness is too precious a pearl to be cast at the feet of the unforgiving; and, without the sincerity that springs from a contrite heart, no man may justly claim mercy." (*Jesus the Christ* [Salt Lake City: Deseret Book Co., 1973], p. 240.)

God asks us to forgive others in order that we ourselves might be blessed. Feelings such as hate, bitterness, revenge, and resentment stop our spiritual growth and make it impossible to receive the guidance and direction of the Holy Ghost. We came here to become like God, yet these feelings are foreign to his nature. Therefore those who nurture these feelings defeat the very purpose of their earth life and become their own worst enemies.

On the other hand, as we develop the power to forgive, we become more like our Father in Heaven and we invite into our lives precious blessings that the unforgiving will never experience. The following story by Elder Dallin H. Oaks illustrates some of the blessings that can accompany the forgiving of others:

> A sister wrote me about her feelings toward a relative who had abused her as a child, leaving her with a painful physical condition. In her words, I have to "live with the pain and try to function around it." She wrote, "At times I [felt] angry and wonder[ed] why I had to suffer the abuse in the first place and why must I continue to pay a price now."
>
> One day, as she listened to a talk in church, her heart was touched. The Spirit bore witness that she should forgive the man who had wronged her and that she could do so with the help of our Lord Jesus Christ. Her letter explained: "The price for that sin has already been paid by Him in Gethsemane. I have no right to hold on to it and demand justice, so I gladly hand it back to Him and rejoice in His love and mercy."
>
> Her letter described the result of her decision: "My heart is so full of joy, peace, and gratitude and love! Isn't His work glorious? How I do love Him! Words cannot express my feelings." ("Modern Pioneers," *Ensign*, November 1989, p. 66.)

In latter-day revelation the Lord has said, "Ye ought to forgive one another; for he that forgiveth not his brother his trespasses standeth condemned before the Lord; for there remaineth in him the greater sin" (D&C 64:9).

There is nothing that anyone can do to us that can have a more damaging effect upon our spiritual well-being than the damage caused by an unforgiving heart. Therefore the greater sin against ourselves is the refusal to forgive, for that limits our happiness and growth. All we have to do is look around us to recognize that feelings of hate, bitterness, and revenge are the companions of unhappiness and misery. They are completely opposite to the feelings of peace, joy, and love that are the fruits of a forgiving heart.

The Savior has asked us not only to forgive but, for our own good, to love those who have offended us. In the Sermon on the Mount, he said:

> Love your enemies, bless them that curse you, do good to them that hate you, and pray for them which despitefully use you, and persecute you;
>
> That ye may be the children of your Father which is in heaven: for he maketh his sun to rise on the evil and on the good, and sendeth rain on the just and on the unjust.
>
> For if ye love them which love you, what reward have ye? do not even the publicans the same?
>
> And if ye salute your brethren only, what do ye more than others? do not even the publicans so? (Matthew 5:44–47.)

President Joseph F. Smith set a wonderful example of how we should feel toward those who have offended us. After discussing the Lord's admonition about forgiving others, President Smith talked about how we should feel toward the enemies of the Church who administer "abuse, insults, slanders, misrepresentations and falsehoods" throughout the land:

> We are willing to risk the judgment of God in these matters in His own due time. We do not propose to keep ourselves eternally in hot water, wrangling, contending, and snarling with our enemies; if we did we should soon become as sour, as vicious, as foul, as low and as

contemptible as they are themselves. Well, do you love them? Now here is the rub! Do you love these slanderers, these liars, these defamers, these persecutors of the innocent and of the unoffending—do you love them? [several voices, No, no.] I can scarcely blame you. [Laughter.] But that is not according to the law of God. I want to tell you how I feel towards them. I love them so much that if I had it in my power to annihilate them from the earth I would not harm a hair of their heads—not one hair of their heads. I love them so well that if I could possibly make them better men, convert them from the error of their ways I would do it, God being my helper. I love them so much that I would not throw a straw in their way to prosperity and happiness, but so far as possible I would hedge up their headlong and downward course to destruction, and yet I detest and abominate their infamous actions and their wicked course. That is how I feel towards them, and that is how much I love them, and if this is not the love that Jesus desired us to have for our enemies, tell me what kind of love we should have for them? (In *Journal of Discourses* 23:284.)

President Smith went on to clarify what types of feelings we should have for those who refuse to respond to our friendship and continue to offend us:

I do not love them so that I would take them into my bosom, or invite them to associate with my family, or that I would give my daughters to their embraces, nor my sons to their counsels. I do not love them so well that I would invite them to the councils of the Priesthood, and the ordinances of the House of God, to scoff and jeer at sacred things which they do not understand . . . ; but I love them so much that I would not hurt them, I would do them good, I would tell the truth about them, I would benefit them if it was in my power, and I would keep them to the utmost of my ability from doing harm to themselves and to their neighbors. I love them that much; but I do not love them with that affection with which I love my wife, my brother, my sister or my friend. There is a difference between the love we should bear towards our enemies and that we should bear towards our friends. . . . We do not love to associate with our enemies, and I do not think the Lord requires us to do it. (Ibid. 23:284–85.)

The Lord not only asks us to forgive our enemies, he asks us to love them—to desire to help them improve their lives and become happier individuals. He requests that we do this not just for them but for ourselves as well. He knows of the havoc and ruin that hate produces in the souls of the unforgiving and asks us to forgive so that we may avoid the bitter fruits of this devastating poison.

These divine principles were clearly illustrated by a man who became known as Wild Bill Cody. Following World War II, a group was assigned to a concentration camp near Wuppertal. They were to obtain medical help for the newly liberated prisoners, who were mostly Jews from Holland, France, and eastern Europe. As the liberators saw what slow starvation had inflicted upon the prisoners, they were overcome with grief and horror. They had arrived too late to help many of the prisoners. In spite of the medicine and food that they brought, scores of the ex-prisoners died each day.

As the liberators worked with the inmates, they came across a Polish man whose name was seven syllables long. Because they could not pronounce his name, and because he had a long, drooping handlebar mustache like the old Western hero's, the American soldiers called him Wild Bill. His mental and physical condition differed dramatically from that of the other inmates. His posture was erect, his eyes were bright, and he was filled with energy.

Because Wild Bill was fluent in English, French, German, Russian, and Polish, he became the unofficial camp translator. The Americans were faced with all kinds of problems in relocating people because many of their families and even whole hometowns had been completely destroyed. Wild Bill worked fifteen and sixteen hours a day helping reunite families, reasoning with the different groups, and counseling forgiveness toward the German soldiers and people.

When one of the liberators commented to him that it was not easy for some to forgive because they had lost family members, Wild Bill related the following story.

We lived in the Jewish section of Warsaw, . . . my wife, our two daughters, and our three little boys. When the Germans reached our street they lined everyone against a wall and opened up with machine guns. I begged to be allowed to die with my family, but because I spoke German they put me in a work group. . . .

I had to decide right then . . . whether to let myself hate the soldiers who had done this. It was an easy decision, really. I was a lawyer. In my practice I had seen too often what hate could do to people's minds and bodies. Hate had just killed the six people who mattered most to me in the world. I decided then that I would spend the rest of my life—whether it was a few days or many years—loving every person I came in contact with. (Quoted in George G. Ritchie, *Return from Tomorrow* [Waco, Texas: Chosen Books, 1978], pp. 115–16; see also p. 114.)

For six years he had lived on the same starvation diet and slept in the same disease-ridden barracks as the other prisoners, yet he had not suffered the physical and mental deterioration that was so prevalent among most of the prisoners. Loving every person was the power that had kept him strong and healthy while many around him had become both physically and spiritually emaciated. Because of his great love for others, every group in the camp considered him a friend and looked to him for help.

The necessity to forgive others is not something that just happens occasionally in our lives. Most of us are presented with situations that call for forgiveness several times a day. The following fictitious example demonstrates some of these situations.

7:00 A.M.—You have been late to work several times recently, so you bought a new alarm clock. Your mate promised to set the alarm but didn't, so you are one hour late for work. Not only are you late but you miss your car pool again and have to waste more money for gas.

9:00 A.M.—When you get to work, your boss chews you out in front of several other employees for being late. He won't listen to your reasons, uses some abrasive and profane language, and tells you that if it happens again, you are through.

10:30 A.M.—A delivery man comes in and asks for the owner of the 1985 Datsun bearing your license-plate number. When you identify yourself, he says that he is sorry but he was backing up and didn't see your car parked in a no-parking zone, where you had left it because you were late and had no place to park. Your car is now about four feet long and resembles an accordion.

11:30 A.M.—You remember that you wouldn't have had the car at work if your mate had set the alarm clock.

5:00 P.M.—When you get home and tell your mate what happened to the car, your mate lets out a groan because he or she had forgotten to mail the insurance and it expired two days ago.

5:15 P.M.—Your eighth-grade son comes home and says that he has lost his glasses at school. He knows that he laid them somewhere on the school lawn while playing football but has completely forgotten where he left them.

5:25 P.M.—Your whole family goes over to the school to hunt for the glasses. You tell everyone to spread out and be very, very careful where they step.

5:26 P.M.—One minute after you stressed the importance of being careful, your nine-year-old son finds the glasses by stepping on them. You now have one pair of glasses in several pieces.

5:35 P.M.—When you arrive back home you find that your supper has burned while the family was looking for the glasses. Your oldest daughter was supposed to have turned down the stove.

5:45 P.M.—A knock sounds on the door, and it is Brother Jones. He says that the bishop expects you to pay $30 into the Scout fund. He's pretty rude about it and wants it now.

6:30 P.M.—You get a phone call from a friend who tells you that a ward member across the street has told people in the ward that you have been stealing items from work and selling them to friends. This is the neighbor that you helped for four hours last Saturday.

7:30 P.M.—You are totally exhausted after the day you have had and decide to do nothing but relax in front of the television set. When you turn it on, you find that the president has called a special news conference. For the next two hours every channel is covering the conference.

9:30 P.M.—After making sure that your alarm clock is set, you kneel down and ask Heavenly Father to help you forgive everyone. You ask him to please help you have a better day tomorrow.

Because we work and live with people who are imperfect, and because we are imperfect ourselves, it is vital to our happiness and peace of mind that we forgive. Not only is forgiveness absolutely necessary in order to obtain a fullness of joy in the next life, but it is essential to our earthly happiness as well. We truly do receive the greater blessing when we forgive offenses against us.

10

Lay Up for Yourselves Treasures in Heaven

MATTHEW 6:10, 19–24

Richard was a seven-year-old boy with no brothers and four older sisters. Since Richard and his sisters were fairly normal, there were times when they argued over which station they would watch on the television set. Because Richard was the smallest and youngest, it isn't difficult to guess who usually lost the arguments. One day the contention became so bad that the father lost his temper and, referring to the television, said, "Look, you five, if I hear one more word I'll chop it up!"

A few days later the father heard a disturbance downstairs. He then heard someone marching up the stairs, and there in his doorway stood a determined little boy. The father explains the discussion that transpired:

> "Dad," he said, "where is your axe?"
> I said, "It's in the furnace room, Rich."
> He said, "Go get it and let's chop it up." I won't repeat the whole conversation, just the headlines from there on.
> I said, "Richard, you really mean it?"
> He said, "Yes, sir."
> I said, "If we do, if we chop this thing up, we are *not* going to get another."
> He said, "I don't care. Let's chop it up."

"Well," I said, "it costs a lot of money. You know those ball games and those nice things we like to watch?"

Yes he knew, but was resolute.

I said, "All right (we went through this awhile), if I said it, I'll do it, and we'll have the greatest ceremony since we buried the frog, but if we do, *if we do,* we will *not* get another. Is that clear?"

"Yes, sir," he said.

"No more ball games, no more movies, no more cartoons."

"Cartoons?" he said. "What is tonight?"

I said, "Friday."

He said, "Is tomorrow Saturday?"

I said, "Yes."

He said, "Could we wait until Monday?"

The father summed up this story by saying: "It gets pretty interesting when it gets personal, doesn't it? When it begins to mean me and my life, my comfort, and my desires, it gets pretty interesting and quite important." (See Marion D. Hanks, *The Banquet of Consequences,* Brigham Young Speeches of the Year [Provo, 3 October 1967], pp. 2–4; emphasis in original.)

Many people are much like young Richard in their approach to living the gospel. They are committed to living all the commandments—starting sometime next week or next month or next year. These are people who consider themselves active in the Church but do not put the things of God first in their lives. Elder Bruce R. McConkie described some of these people as follows:

> Their interests are largely centered in temporal things, in making a living, in the things of this world. They are not wicked and ungodly in the sense of being carnal and evil. But they are not devoting their energies to the spread of truth and the perfecting of the lives of their brethren. They are probably part tithepayers, and they likely go to sacrament meeting and perform church service when it is convenient. They seek the honors of men and the wealth of the world with more zeal than they do the honors of God and the riches of eternity. They are lukewarm and their souls will not be saved. (*Doctrinal New Testament Commentary,* 3 vols. [Salt Lake City: Bookcraft, 1965–73], 3:460.)

It is not that these people do not think of God or even serve him. Their problem is that there are other things in their lives that they consider to be more important. One of the most significant things we can ever do is establish proper priorities. Notice how quickly the telegraph operator in the following story changes his priorities when he realizes his future is in jeopardy:

> A railroad tycoon became lost in the mountains, and only by great good fortune was he able to find his way out of the hills. He discovered (of all things) a rail line that led him (of all places) to a small shack which turned out to be an outpost of his own railroad. Filled with joy at the great reprieve of life he had received, he went into the shack suffused with good will, only to have his newly won appreciation turn into distress because it was as cold inside as out. Only in a sequestered corner was it warm, and in that corner a man sat, the one-man operator of this outpost station, tapping out telegrams on the key.
>
> The tycoon became annoyed at the fact that it was warm only in this little secluded area to which he had no access, and said to the man impatiently, "Why don't you build a fire in this place so people can stay warm?" The man, not knowing whom he was talking to, of course, said, "Look, bud, I'm too busy sending wires to build fires." The railroad president took his card, reached for a telegraph blank, and wrote a little message, put his card with the blank across the counter and waited. The railroad telegrapher read the message which was "By return wire, fire this man," and looked at the card, gulped, and disappeared. He came back a few minutes later into the larger area of the room with his arms loaded with kindling and coal. The railroad president said, "Did you send that wire?" He said, "Look, sir, I'm too busy building fires to send wires." (Marion D. Hanks, *Was He Relevant?* Brigham Young University Speeches of the Year [Provo, 17 December 1968], pp. 1–2.)

God has revealed to us that his first priority is to help us obtain immortality and eternal life (see Moses 1:39). However, until this becomes our most important priority, we will never receive the great blessings associated with eternal life. Jesus was trying to help us establish our priorities when he said, "Lay not up for yourselves treasures upon earth, where moth and rust doth corrupt, and where thieves break through and steal: but lay up for yourselves treasures in heaven, where neither moth nor rust doth corrupt, and where thieves do not break through nor steal: for where your treasure is, there will your heart be also" (Matthew 6:19–21).

On a Sunday morning several years ago, a member was attending church when someone rushed in and told him that his house was on fire. He quickly rounded up his two sons, ages twelve and sixteen, and they headed for his ranch. The man was worried about his wife, who had stayed home because of recent surgery, but the crew of a returning fire truck stopped them and told them that she was okay.

They had just finished building the home of their dreams, and it had become a great source of pleasure to the whole family. As they approached the top of a hill, they could see the smoke coming from their new home. Relating this experience, the father said: "We could tell that our home was completely engulfed in flames; and I just stopped the car at the top of the hill for a few minutes. I said to my sons, 'Now look, you can spend all your life storing up treasures of the earth, and you can sit on a hill and watch them go up in flames, or, you can store up the right kind of treasures and take them with you through eternity.'" (Quoted in Rex D. Pinegar, "Home First," *Ensign,* May 1990, p. 11.)

The treasures of the earth include such things as wealth, clothes, homes, money, property, and other physical possessions. Earthly treasures also include such things as special honors bestowed by men, recognition from social organizations and affiliations, position and power in the workplace, and political and social positions. Since none of these things have much eternal value, it is a costly mistake to place any one of them first in our lives.

On the other hand, there are things we can purchase with our time, effort, and money here upon the earth that can be taken with us when we leave this earth. Some of these treasures were listed by Elder Bruce R. McConkie:

While yet on earth men may lay up treasures in heaven. These treasures, earned here and now in mortality, are in effect deposited to our eternal bank account in heaven where eventually they will be reinherited again in immortality. Treasures in heaven are the character, perfections, and attributes which men acquire by obedience to law. Thus, those who gain such attributes of godliness as knowledge, faith, justice, judgment, mercy, and truth, will find these same attributes restored to them again in immortality. (*Doctrinal New Testament Commentary,* 1:239.)

The development of character and the formation of Godlike qualities such as mercy, patience, and love takes more than a partial involvement in the gospel of Christ—it takes a total commitment to the Lord and his purposes. It takes complete cooperation with God in the development of our own soul. As Elder McConkie taught in the previous quote, this soul-growth comes from obedience to God's law. Jesus submitted fully and willingly to the will of the Father, and we must do the same if we are to lay up for ourselves the same treasures and blessings that Jesus enjoys. After discussing the Savior's commitment to His Father, BYU president Jeffrey R. Holland said:

Frankly, I am a bit haunted by the thought that this is the first and most important thing he may want to know about *us* when we meet him one day in similar fashion. Did *we* obey, even if it was painful? Did *we* submit, even if the cup was bitter indeed? Did we yield to a vision higher and holier than our own, even when we may have seen no vision in it at all?

One by one he invites us to feel the wounds in his hands and his feet and his side. And as we pass and touch and wonder, perhaps he whispers, "If any man will come after me, let him deny himself, and take up his cross, and follow me" (Matthew 16:24). . . .

. . . Education, or public service, or social responsibility, or professional accomplishment of *any* kind is in vain if we cannot, in those crucial moments of pivotal personal history, submit ourselves to God even when all our hopes and fears may tempt us otherwise. We must be willing to place all that we have—not just our possessions (they may be the easiest things of all to give up), but also our

ambition and pride and stubbornness and vanity—we must place it
all on the altar of God, kneel there in silent submission, and willingly
walk away. ("The Will of the Father in All Things," in *Brigham
Young University 1988–89 Devotional and Fireside Speeches* [Provo:
Brigham Young University Press, 1989], pp. 77, 78; emphasis in
original.)

This type of commitment was demonstrated by a young
Pakistani naval officer who was sent to the United States for special training. While there he associated with some members of the
Church who referred him to the missionaries. He learned about
the Savior and the great atonement that had been wrought in his
behalf. He was told about Joseph Smith and the marvelous visita-
tion that he received from the Father and the Son. The young
officer accepted the gospel and was baptized into the Lord's
church.

Just before returning home to his native country, he had the
opportunity of speaking with Elder Gordon B. Hinckley. When
Elder Hinckley asked him what would happen to him when he
returned home as a Christian and especially as a Mormon
Christian, he replied: "My family will cast me out. They will
regard me as dead. As for my fate in the Pakistani navy, I can
expect no advancement. In fact, I shall likely be broken in rank.
My future has been foreclosed."

When Elder Hinckley asked him if he was willing to pay so
great a price for the gospel, the young man's eyes filled with tears
and he answered, "It's true, isn't it?"

When Elder Hinckley affirmed that it was true, the young
officer responded, "Then what else matters?" (See *It's True, Isn't
It?* Brigham Young University Speeches of the Year [Provo, 14
December 1971], p. 1.)

When we choose to follow Christ with all our heart, mind, and
strength, we choose to be changed. "No man," said President
David O. McKay, "can sincerely resolve to apply to his daily life
the teachings of Jesus of Nazareth without sensing a change in his
own nature" (in *Conference Report*, April 1962, p. 7). This change

is referred to in the scriptures as being born again. Through the atonement of Christ and by yielding to the enticings of the Spirit, we put off the natural man and become a new creature—one with Christlike motives and desires. We become submissive, meek, humble, patient, full of love, and willing to submit to the Lord in all things (see Mosiah 3:19). Our desires to sin are replaced with a desire to do good continually (see Mosiah 5:2). Our lives always become more joyful and meaningful as we place the things of God ahead of the things of the world, because the things of God are the true source of peace and joy. As the blessings that follow obedience fill our lives and hearts, we soon realize that the sacrifices we thought we were making were really just investments in things of much greater worth.

11

Every Good Tree Bringeth Forth Good Fruit

MATTHEW 7:17–20

There is a sickness or syndrome that seriously affects some members of the Church. This syndrome keeps them from developing the attributes that will lead to greater peace and happiness. Elder Jacob de Jager once described this syndrome:

> Some members, after being baptized into this church, have the mistaken idea that they have stepped on an escalator that will carry them smoothly and automatically to heaven. They think that all they have to do is hang on to the iron rod, which they conceive as the handrail of the escalator that moves up and up with them to heaven. . . . That's what Elder Maxwell calls the escalator syndrome, and I thought you should be aware of that. There are no escalators in this kingdom. ("Perfecting the Saints," in *Brigham Young University 1988–89 Devotional and Fireside Speeches* [Provo: Brigham Young University Press, 1989], p. 88.)

Many of those who suffer from this syndrome have the mistaken idea that keeping the commandments saves them. They feel that church attendance will save them, that the payment of tithing will save them, that regular home teaching will save them. They have not understood that the commandments are only a means to an end—not the end itself.

Jesus indicated that we need to be born again in order to be saved. Being born again is much more than entering the waters of baptism and receiving a confirmation from the hands of the priesthood. President Ezra Taft Benson said that "in addition to the physical ordinance of baptism and the laying on of hands, one must be spiritually born again to gain exaltation and eternal life." He taught that "the world would shape human behavior, but Christ can change human nature." ("Born of God," *Ensign,* July 1989, pp. 2, 4.)

Alma taught that those who are born again are "changed from their carnal and fallen state, to a state of righteousness" (Mosiah 27:25). By obeying the Lord's commandments and responding to the quiet whisperings of the Spirit, our very natures can be changed. We can literally put off the natural man and become spiritual in nature. This cannot be accomplished alone but can happen only as we allow Christ to have complete control of our hearts. Our desires will be swallowed up in his desires, and unholy thoughts and cravings will be purged from our souls. Moroni taught that this spiritual birth is not achieved alone: "Come unto Christ, and be perfected in him, and deny yourselves of all ungodliness; and if ye shall deny yourselves of all ungodliness, and love God with all your might, mind and strength, then is his grace sufficient for you, that by his grace ye may be perfect in Christ; and if by the grace of God ye are perfect in Christ, ye can in nowise deny the power of God" (Moroni 10:32).

When we turn our hearts over to God, we begin to see the fruits of the Spirit that are mentioned throughout the scriptures. In the Sermon on the Mount, Jesus taught that people can be judged by their fruits: "Ye shall [recognize] them by their fruits. Do men gather grapes of thorns, or figs of thistles? Even so every good tree bringeth forth good fruit; but a corrupt tree bringeth forth evil fruit. . . . Wherefore by their fruits ye shall know them." (Matthew 7:16–17, 20.)

The Greek words for *good fruit* carry the meaning of beautiful, precious fruit without blemish. Church attendance, scripture study, prayer, and other religious acts are not the fruit itself but fertilizers, if you will, that nourish the fruit and help it grow. The fruit is actually the traits and blessings that come to us through the Spirit as we give our heart and soul to God. Paul described some of these fruits: "But the fruit of the Spirit is love, joy, peace, longsuffering, gentleness, goodness, faith, meekness, temperance: against such there is no law" (Galatians 5:22–23).

We did not come to earth just so we could go to church or pay our tithing or attend the temple. Our purpose here is to become like our Father in Heaven so we can enjoy all that he has. When we stand before God, what we have done will not be as important as what we have become. If this is not understood, we may become complacent with our membership and feel that our church activity will save us.

The scriptures make it clear that we cannot develop the attributes of God without his help. Being willing to do whatever the Lord asks of us and striving to live the gospel put us in a position where we can receive help from the Lord. One writer explained it this way:

> Through the Holy Ghost, the Atonement makes possible certain spiritual endowments that actually purify our nature and enable us to live a more "eternal" or Godlike life. . . . Then we will exhibit divine character not just because we think we should, but because that is the way we are.
>
> The gift of *charity* illustrates this process. . . . This love . . . is not developed entirely by our own power, even though our faithfulness is a necessary qualification to receive it. Rather, charity is "*bestowed* upon" the "true followers" of Christ. (Moro. 7:48.) Its source, like all other blessings of the Atonement, is the grace of God. . . .
>
> The purpose of the endowment of charity is not merely to cause Christ's followers to engage in charitable acts toward others, desirable as that is. The ultimate purpose is to transform his followers to become *like him:* "he hath bestowed [this love] upon all who are true

followers of his Son, . . . that when he shall appear we shall be like him." (Moro. 7:48.) (Bruce C. Hafen, "Beauty For Ashes: The Atonement of Jesus Christ" *Ensign,* April 1990, p. 12; emphasis in original.)

The importance of giving God not just our minds but our hearts was demonstrated by a convert to the Church named Mollie Sorensen. When she stood to bear her testimony for the first time, it went something like this: "I know the gospel is true. It is so reasonable and logical. The principles seem right and natural, and they answer questions I have had all my life." Mollie had an intellectual testimony but had few *feelings* about the doctrines of the kingdom. She was so fascinated with "hearing and talking about the word that [she] had neglected much of the doing." As her knowledge continued to outpace her ability to live the gospel, she become confused and discouraged. She felt inferior to some of the members who seemed to understand the gospel less yet live it better.

Mollie's life began to change for the better when she became friends with Elaine. Mollie was surprised and disturbed when Elaine told her that she prayed about such simple things as Primary lessons, problems with her children, and lost car keys. Mollie had always felt that God couldn't be bothered with her petty problems because he had so many other things to worry about. Since it was apparent that God was answering Elaine's prayers, Mollie began to feel that God must love Elaine more than her. She explains what happened next:

> In time I realized that, if God was no respecter of persons, there could be only one explanation for the phenomenon I saw in Elaine's life: Elaine was paying a price that I was not. While I was satisfied merely to know that God existed, she leaned on him for guidance and help. While I excluded him from my everyday life, she invited him daily to be part of hers. While I viewed him as the great author of principles and creator of the universe, she knew him also as her own Father. In short, while I was giving all my mind to him, she was also giving her heart.

I knew that I needed to begin a new phase of the conversion process. In the first phase, I had discovered principles of truth; now I hoped to find the Man of truth. . . .

In prayer, I invited Heavenly Father to be a part of my life. And in time, as I learned to share more openly the concerns of my heart, he drew near. When I prayed for help with a Primary lesson, I received insights I had never had before. When I prayed for help with my temper, my anger left. When I prayed to overcome my inclination to criticize my husband, I forgot the reason for my criticism. Over and over, tiny miracles occurred; over and over, I marveled that God would care!

In this second phase of my conversion, I discovered that God not only exists, he lives! Through his tender care, I could now stand and testify: "Yes, the gospel is true, but even more important, *He* is true—and real and loving and personal and powerful. Our Father has not merely given us the truth and organization of the Church. He will give of himself, if we but ask." (Mollie Hobaugh Sorensen, "Learning Faith," *Ensign,* March 1985, pp. 24–27.)

Once Mollie decided to give her heart to God, he was able to enter into her life and help her become more like him. Her basic nature began to change for the better. Sometimes we forget we are of divine parentage and lose sight of why we are here. A seven-year-old girl related the following experience:

I was practicing the piano one day, and it made me cry because it was so bad. Then I decided to practice ballet, and it made me cry more; it was bad, too. So then I decided to draw a picture because I knew I could do that good, but it was horrid. Of course it made me cry.

Then my little three-year-old brother came up, and I said, "Duffy, what *can* I be? What can *I* be? I can't be a piano player or an artist or a ballet girl. What can I be?" He came up to me and whispered, "You can be my sister." (Quoted in Patricia T. Holland, "Filling the Measure of Your Creation," in *Brigham Young University 1988–89 Devotional and Fireside Speeches,* p. 71; emphasis in original.)

When we become discouraged and begin to think that life is tougher than we are, it may help us to remember that we are a member of God's family. We may not be able to do many things well, but we can be a good brother or sister to those around us, and we can become more like our Father because we are his children. As with Mollie and Elaine, the key to our spiritual growth is to invite our Father into our lives. Without his help—his guidance and power—we will never develop his nature and attributes, but with his help we will be astounded at the progress we make. As we see the fruits of the Spirit maturing and ripening in our lives, we will feel the joy that comes from living and being more like our Heavenly Parents.

12

It Fell Not: For It Was Founded upon a Rock

MATTHEW 7:21, 24–27

Where would you rank Jesus on the list of people who have had the greatest effect on the course of human history? In a book entitled *The 100: A Ranking of History's Most Influential Persons,* Jesus was listed not first but third. The author's reason for ranking Jesus third casts a serious reflection on the Christian world: "The impact of Jesus on human history is so obvious and so enormous that few people would question his placement near the top of the list. Indeed, the more likely question is why Jesus . . . has not been placed first. . . . [His teachings are] surely among the most remarkable and original ethical ideas ever presented. If they were widely followed, I would have no hesitation in placing Jesus first in this book." (Michael H. Hart [Secaucus, New Jersey: Citadel Press, 1987], pp. 47, 50.)

After quoting Mr. Hart, Elder Rex D. Pinegar commented: "What a searing and likely very true observation: If Jesus' teachings were widely followed, Mr. Hart would have no hesitation in placing Jesus first! With these thoughts in mind, I feel it is appropriate for us to ask, 'Where do we rank Jesus Christ in our lives? Does He come first, as He should?' Perhaps a more significant question would be, 'Where would we rank ourselves as *followers* of Jesus' teachings?' Do we live as Christians in word and deed?" (Rex D.

Pinegar, "Follow Christ in Word and Deed," *Ensign,* November 1991, p. 39.)

The importance of being doers, not just believers, was emphasized by the Lord when he stated that "not every one that saith unto me, Lord, Lord, shall enter into the kingdom of heaven; but he that doeth the will of my Father which is in heaven" (Matthew 7:21).

Although most Church members are acquainted with the parable about the wise man who built his house upon the rock, many do not know what made the man wise. When more than 150 members were asked what the wise man did that caused his house to be built upon rock and what the foolish man did that caused his house to be built upon sand, not one of them knew the answer. As you read this parable, please notice what made one man wise and the other one foolish.

> Therefore whosoever heareth these sayings of mine, *and doeth them,* I will liken him unto a wise man, which built his house upon a rock:
>
> And the rain descended, and the floods came, and the winds blew, and beat upon that house; and it fell not: for it was founded upon a rock.
>
> And every one that heareth these sayings of mine, *and doeth them not,* shall be likened unto a foolish man, which built his house upon the sand:
>
> And the rain descended, and the floods came, and the winds blew, and beat upon that house; and it fell: and great was the fall of it. (Matthew 7:24–27; emphasis added.)

The wise man heard the sayings of Jesus and *did them* while the foolish man heard the sayings of Jesus but *did them not.* Obedience is the foundation that gives us the stability we need to overcome the daily press of trials, tribulations, and temptations. On one conference visit to California, President Harold B. Lee was approached by numerous parents who wondered if they should move to the Salt Lake Valley in order to get away from the negative influences that were crowding in upon them. In response, he emphasized the importance of obedience:

> Now the all-important thing for you folks is *not where you live,* because you cannot escape the power of evil; but the all-important thing is *how you live.* If you folks want to be protected during this time of stress, you have given you in the gospel of Jesus Christ the fundamental principles by which you can be saved. . . .
> . . . You can do that right here in California. You don't have to move into the Salt Lake Valley, because you won't be protected any more there than here if you don't keep the commandments of God. (Address at Brigham Young University Sixth Stake conference, 27 April 1969.)

James pointed out that where there is no obedience, our faith is useless: "Faith without works is dead" (James 2:20). He reminded us that even the devils believe in God. It is obedience that opens the windows of heaven and allows us to receive the divine blessings that we desire. President Spencer W. Kimball explained the relationship between obedience and blessings:

> Even the most demanding labor unions would hardly ask the wages before the labor. But many of us would have the vigor without the observance of the health laws, prosperity through the opened windows of heaven without the payment of our tithes. We would have the close communion with our Father without fasting and praying; we would have rain in due season and peace in the land without observing the Sabbath and keeping the other commandments of the Lord. We would pluck the rose before planting the roots; we would harvest the grain before sowing and cultivating. (*Faith Precedes the Miracle* [Salt Lake City: Deseret Book Co., 1972], p. 4.)

Obedience is an outer manifestation of the inner love and appreciation we feel for our Heavenly Father and for the Savior. Almost daily the world attempts to teach us that actions have little to do with love. Movies and television shows often depict a husband who is having extramarital affairs with numerous women. When his wife finally becomes aware of his disloyalty and confronts him with it, he invariably tells her that he really loves her and asks her to forgive him. This of course is a bunch of hogwash. When a man truly loves his wife, he is faithful to her and does everything he can to make her happy.

The same principle is true about our love for Heavenly Father and the Savior. Jesus said "He that hath my commandments and *keepeth them,* he it is that loveth me" (John 14:21; emphasis added). We may claim that we love God, but our actions are a true indication of the depth of our love. Jesus has promised those who obey his words that he and the Father will come to them and make their abode with them (see John 14:23). Obedience brings the guidance and direction of God into our lives.

Our obedience indicates that we are individuals of honesty and integrity. Rex E. Lee, as president of Brigham Young University, taught the link between obedience and integrity when he addressed the importance of BYU faculty members and students obeying the school's honor code:

> For citizens of BYU, faculty and students alike, all parts of our honor code rise to the level of moral principles. The reason is that each of us, prior to and as a condition of our employment or enrollment here, made a promise, a covenant, to keep and obey those standards. The moral principle, therefore, rises above and exists apart from the intrinsic merit of skirt lengths, or hair lengths, or shorts, or beards. It is a matter of integrity, of complying with what we promised to do. And whether we agree or disagree with given aspects of the dress and grooming standards is irrelevant to that commitment. ("Where Much Is Given: Some Thoughts on Appreciation," in *Brigham Young University 1989–90 Devotional and Fireside Speeches* [Provo: Brigham Young University Press, 1990], p. 28.)

Our membership in the Lord's kingdom and church is the same. When we were baptized, we made the commitment that we would do our very best to keep all the commandments. Now that we have given our word, our integrity is on the line. Obedience demonstrates that we are men and women of integrity, and dis-obedience—especially deliberate disobedience—indicates that our word means little to us.

By living obedient lives, we demonstrate to the Lord that he can place his trust in us. We tell him by our actions that he can rely upon us even in difficult situations and circumstances. The type of loyalty and obedience we need to develop is illustrated in the following story:

> The Arab thought as much of his mount as he did of his children. . . . The horse was the pride of the family, and his development was watched and guided with the greatest love in the world.
>
> . . . Note one thing about this animal's training. They deter-mined that he should in very deed be a thoroughbred. When the colt is a few months old, they ring a bell and push the little fellow over to his master's tent. . . . They repeat that operation until in a few weeks the intelligent fellow automatically, when he hears the bell ring, turns right about, no matter what he is doing and trots off to his master's headquarters.
>
> But the day of testing is coming—a day, if you please, when his mettle will be tried—a test to determine whether they've raised fif-teen hundred pounds of horseflesh or a creature to be labeled a "thoroughbred." Well, just what do they do with him; how do they determine his worth? Now watch—here are the details of the exami-nation: He's now going to get a diploma or be labeled a cull.
>
> The horse is now about three years old. They have rung this bell every day, and he hasn't missed a perfect response—not a hesitation at the sound of the gong, a beeline to the tent of his master. But so far no great sacrifice has been asked of him, but on this day of exam it's going to be different. They keep him . . . away from water for three days—his tongue is as thick as leather. That third day he's done everything but jump over the fence to water. While in this des-perate condition, when everything is ready, they let down the bars of the corral. He leaps like a deer—when he's half way to water, they ring the bell. If he continues his run for water, he's a cull. If he turns

right about to his master's tent, he's a thoroughbred, and he is sent over the ocean and to the ends of the earth, as may be demanded. (Marvin O. Ashton, *To Whom It May Concern* [Salt Lake City: Bookcraft, 1946], pp. 234–35.)

For those who love the Lord and desire to serve him, their obedience becomes as natural to them as the thoroughbred race-horse responding to the bell. It becomes as much a part of them as breathing and speaking. We have thousands of opportunities to be obedient every day. Every time we help another person or stand up for the right or say a kind word, we are demonstrating our obedience. Each time we pray or study the scriptures or attend a church meeting, we are showing our love for our Father in Heaven. Each good thought and every good deed that we perform draws us closer to God and makes it more possible for us to receive guidance and direction from him. Obedience is simply a way of life—a way of living as God would live if he were here. As we come to obey God in all things, our spiritual foundation is strengthened until, with the help of the Lord, we can resist all temptation and overcome all opposition. Truly it is a wise man or woman who builds his or her life on the rock of obedience.

13

My Peace I Give unto You

JOHN 14:27

The funeral was an unusually sad one. A young mother had died in childbirth, leaving four small children to be cared for by the father. Even though the funeral talks had been meaningful and expressive, many people in the congregation still felt feelings of bitterness and resentment. They questioned why a loving Heavenly Father would allow such a cruel thing to happen to such a righteous family.

When the formal part of the program was over, the young father, sensing the heavy spirit that was present, quietly walked to the pulpit and said: "I sense your grief and concern, . . . but there is something I should tell you to comfort you. The first hour after my wife's death I didn't know how I could possibly stand it—how I could possibly go on without her. But then a sweet, peaceful spirit filled my soul, and since then I have had the assurance that everything will be all right. Don't worry about us, we're going to be just fine."

These simple words of faith and humility brought the Spirit of the Lord into the meeting, and feelings of bitterness and doubt were replaced with comfort and peace. As the father shared the spiritual comfort he had received, the Spirit descended upon the congregation and everyone went home comforted. (See Spencer J. Condie, "Thy Constant Companion," *Ensign,* October 1980, p. 33.)

The peace that this young father received is one of the greatest blessings God offers us, and it is available to all of us. During
his mortal ministry, Jesus promised us spiritual comfort and
peace:

> Come unto me, all ye that labour and are heavy laden, and I will
> give you rest.
>
> Take my yoke upon you, and learn of me; for I am meek and
> lowly in heart: and ye shall find rest unto your souls. (Matthew
> 11:28–29.)

> Peace I leave with you, my peace I give unto you: not as the
> world giveth, give I unto you. Let not your heart be troubled, nei-
> ther let it be afraid. (John 14:27.)

This peace that the Lord promises is much more than physical
peace. It is an inner peace that can exist even when we are surrounded by external conflict. An editorial from the *Church News*
describes the great power that the Lord's peace offers us in our
present world of dissension and strife:

> He gives peace to the soul. And He gives it not through massive
> conquests on great battlefields or sparingly to only a chosen few, but
> to all men, women and children—one by one—as they place their
> trust and faith in Him.
>
> We know the peace Jesus offers as tranquility of the soul, or
> inner peace. It is mighty and powerful. It is indestructible and
> immune to the actions of others. It can endure all calamity, every
> disaster, all manner of turmoil. It enables individuals to rise above
> whatever tumult surrounds them. (19 December 1992, p. 16.)

Consider, just for a moment, the great power of this peace
that Jesus offers us. It can resist any and every problem that arises
through our daily living. When we place our trust in the Savior
and strive to follow in his footsteps, his peace can help us through
every negative situation that we face. This peace can transcend

feelings of hate, bitterness, discouragement, disappointment, loneliness, fear, and all other feelings that keep us from enjoying life and hoping for a better future. Patsy Mitchell bears testimony of the importance and power of the Savior's peace:

> I am beginning a new life. For nearly eight years polio has left me confined to a wheel chair with only ten percent muscle restoration. To me this is a new life because I understand why I am afflicted and what my mission is in this life. I realize now how wonderful the blessings which are taken for granted.
>
> Have you ever thought what a blessing it is to breathe? Well, I didn't until I was imprisoned within an iron lung for weeks and weeks. I vowed that if I ever could breathe alone again, I wouldn't ever take one breath of air for granted. I'm so happy that after all I've been through, I can breathe by myself. A new-found gift God has given me is *peace of mind*. With peace of mind God is with me and when he is with me, I cannot fail.
>
> When I think of all my blessings, I am greatly humbled. God gave me eyes with which to see; he gave me ears with which to hear; he gave me intelligence with which to reason. With these gifts I can see the wonders of nature and hear the beautiful music I love so much. I can read a book and understand. . . .
>
> When I received my Patriarchal Blessing the Lord promised many wonderful things; but only if I accomplish my mission. He sent me here for a purpose and that is to make people happy and help them to realize all they have to be thankful for.
>
> Even with only ten percent of my muscles restored, I have been blessed to do all I came here to do, but it has not been easy. I have had to work very hard to make these muscles work. I have been blessed to develop my ability to draw and paint. I can play the lovely church hymns on the piano when my arms are propped up. I have written a book about my eighteen years of life, and about the testimony I have gained. ("God Gave Me Eyes," *Improvement Era*, July 1960, *The Era of Youth* section, p. 9; emphasis added.)

This peace that Patsy enjoys comes only through Christ. The night before his crucifixion Jesus told his apostles that *in him* they might have peace. He explained that in the world they would face tribulation but that they should "be of good cheer" because he had overcome the world (John 16:33).

Val Johnson is another person who has received this loving gift of peace from the Savior. Just a few minutes after a new daughter had been born to Val and his wife, Dora, they were told that she had Down's syndrome. Val humbly shares how the Lord brought peace to his heart:

> The next few days were difficult. Dora and I struggled with the usual terrible questions: Why us? What did we do wrong? There was an emptiness in our hearts, an aching need for some kind of assurance that Someone was in control.
>
> One night, numb with worry and tired of asking questions my mind knew the answers to but which my heart refused to acknowledge, I asked Heavenly Father for some peace. Just peace.
>
> And it came, washing over me in waves of joy. With that peace came a scene to my mind I have thought much about since. It wasn't a vision. It was simply a scenario that impressed itself on my consciousness gently but firmly.

In his mind, Val saw himself with a group of friends in the premortal existence. The plan of salvation had been presented to them, and they were discussing the plan with one another when Heavenly Father and the Savior joined their group. Heavenly Father explained to them they were going to be a family on earth and that one of them was going to receive a mind and body with "capacities different from the others'." He stated that this person would not be able to experience life as fully as the others but that she would help the rest of the family learn "how to love purely and unconditionally."

Following this announcement, the group was silent, and it seemed as if Heavenly Father was waiting for something. Val found himself fearing that this mission might fall to him. Then the "brightest and most beautiful" person among the group stepped forward and said, "Here am I. Send me." This person was their Down's syndrome child, Jenny.

Val doesn't really know whether or not this scene actually took place, but he does know that the principle he learned from it is true: "Jenny is a child of God, a goddess in embryo, and we have much of life and love to learn from each other."

When Jenny was eleven years old, Val shared what he had learned from his association with Jenny and from the Lord: "Happiness, soul-deep happiness, has little to do with outward circumstances. It has everything to do with inner peace. And that peace comes when our lives are so in harmony with the Lord's that the Holy Spirit can heal our broken hearts and make us whole. Inseparably connected to the Spirit of God, we can then claim our birthright—that peace, that joy which passes all understanding." (R. Val Johnson, "The Purpose of Life," *Ensign,* April 1993, p. 27.)

The peace that Spencer, Patsy, and Val received comes as we strive to do good. Paul taught that peace comes "to every man that worketh good" (Romans 2:10). He taught that the conveyer of peace is the Holy Spirit: "But the fruit of the Spirit is love, joy, peace, longsuffering, gentleness, goodness, faith, meekness, [and] temperance" (Galatians 5:22–23).

Only those who have felt this peace realize how wonderful and powerful it really is, for "the peace of God . . . passeth all understanding" (Philippians 4:7). Whether we are faced with death or divorce, war or a wayward child, sickness or financial pressures, we can receive this peace. To his Latter-Day Saints the Lord has promised that those who do "the works of righteousness shall receive [their] reward, even peace in this world, and eternal life in the world to come" (D&C 59:23).

14

The Parable of the Sower
MATTHEW 13:1–23

After twenty months of teaching, Jesus began to teach in parables. His first parable, the parable of the sower, is of great relevance in our lives because it identifies attitudes that govern our spiritual growth and, therefore, our peace and happiness. In this parable a sower goes forth to sow. Today we place the seeds directly into the soil, but in those days they tossed the seeds in front of them haphazardly to the ground. Therefore some of the seeds in the parable fell by the wayside. Others fell in stony places, among thorns, or upon good ground. The seeds represent the word of God, and the soils represent four types of hearts and how receptive they are to the word of God. The seeds are good, therefore whether or not they bring forth fruit is determined by the soil. Each one of us is represented by one of the soils in the parable. It would be beneficial for all of us to examine our own hearts and our accessibility and obedience to the word of God.

The parable states that "a sower went forth to sow; and when he sowed, some seeds fell by the way side, and the fowls came and devoured them up" (Matthew 13:3–4). Roads and pathways went directly through many fields, and this constant traffic made the surface of these areas too hard for seed to take root.

This type of soil represents those who are referred to as hard-hearted in the scriptures. They are not seeking the word of God and refuse to listen to the promptings of the Spirit. The more they reject the Spirit and God's word, the harder their hearts become. Missionaries often run across this type of soil as they proselyte from door to door.

One man who was contacted by missionaries said that he was a very religious person and was seeking the word of God. As the missionaries discussed a certain aspect of the gospel with this man, he rejected it completely. He said that he would believe it only if it was taught in *his* Bible. When the missionaries located the concept in his Bible, he ripped out the page, crumpled it up, and threw it onto the floor. He then stated that the idea was no longer taught in his Bible. Because of the hardness of his heart, the seed or the word of God could not take root.

Another man claimed that he sincerely wanted to know the truthfulness of the Book of Mormon. He claimed that he had been reading it and praying about it for several weeks but had not received an answer from the Spirit. In response to questions from the missionaries, he said that he read and prayed about the Book of Mormon each morning at about 9:00.

About 9:30 the next morning the missionaries stopped by his home to see if they could help him with his study of the Book of Mormon. To their chagrin, he was not reading the Book of Mormon but instead was reading a pornographic magazine. As they conversed with him, they found out that he read the Book of Mormon each day for four or five minutes, offered a quick prayer, and then spent the rest of the morning reading pornography. This man was doing nothing to soften his heart so the word of God could take root.

Another man claimed that he had proven the Book of Mormon was false. When asked how he had performed this great miracle, he said that he had knelt down and asked God to strike him dead if the Book of Mormon was true. Therefore the Book of Mormon had to be false because he was still alive.

Few of us are as hard-hearted as these three people, but some of us may be resistive to the Spirit in some areas. When we become selective about which commandments we will obey and which part of the prophets' counsel we will accept, we limit some of the fruits of the Spirit that we could otherwise enjoy.

Jesus described the second type of soil in the following words: "Some [seed] fell upon stony places, where they had not much earth; and forthwith they sprung up; and when the sun was up, they were scorched, because they had no deepness of earth; and because they had no root, they withered away" (JST, Matthew 13:5).

This soil represents the person who "heareth the word and readily with joy receiveth it, yet hath not root in *himself*, and endureth but for a while; for when tribulation or persecution ariseth because of the word, by and by he is offended" (JST, Matthew 13:19; emphasis added).

A family that we will refer to as the Larson family illustrates this second type of soil. Brother and Sister Larson had been married for fifteen years and had been blessed with two sons and a daughter. They had made sure that their children were blessed and baptized but had not actively participated in the Church since their marriage. With the prompting of some neighbors that they were friends with, they decided to learn more about the Church and were taught the basic missionary lessons by stake missionaries. They accepted the gospel teachings with joy and made the decision to prepare themselves so they could be sealed in the temple. They became very active, and after a few months Brother Larson was called to be the elders quorum president. Then the day arrived when they knelt across the altar in the temple, along with their three children, and participated in the ordinance that could make them an eternal family unit.

Two or three months later they stopped coming to church and refused to tell anyone what the problem was. Eventually Brother Larson admitted that someone in the ward had offended them and they had decided to no longer be involved with the Church. Many ward friends tried to change their minds but to no avail. They started smoking and drinking again, became unfaithful to each other, and eventually lost everything, both physically and spiritually, that they had once possessed.

The Savior taught in the parable that the word of God must take *root in us*. Their problem was that they never did those things that would cause the word of God to take root in their hearts. In times of tribulation or persecution, someone else's testimony or encouragement is not enough. We need to have the seeds of the gospel planted deep within our own hearts. Alma taught that it takes time and effort to get this spiritual depth:

> But if ye will nourish the word, yea, nourish the tree as it begin-neth to grow, by your faith with great diligence, and with patience, looking forward to the fruit thereof, it shall take root; and behold it shall be a tree springing up unto everlasting life.
>
> And because of your diligence and your faith and your patience with the word in nourishing it, that it may take root *in you,* behold, by and by ye shall pluck the fruit thereof. (Alma 32:41–42; emphasis added.)

Joseph Smith taught that the "things of God are of deep import; and time, and experience, and careful and ponderous and solemn thoughts can only find them out" (*History of the Church,* 3:295).

Describing a third type of soil, Jesus said that some seed "fell among thorns, and the thorns grew up, and choked it, and it yielded no fruit" (Mark 4:7). Some people accept the gospel but allow worldly cares, pleasures, riches, and lusts to choke the word, so they bring forth "no fruit to perfection" (see Mark 4:18–19; Luke 8:14).

In this type of soil, the plant does not die—it just loses its strength to produce fruit. Two or three years ago a young couple planted a large garden behind their rental home. Just about the time the plants began to grow well, they had to leave town for five weeks. While they were gone, it rained often and the plants received plenty of moisture, but no one was around to take care of the weeds. When they returned, the weeds were four feet tall and their mature corn was eighteen inches tall. Most of the nutri-ents that the corn needed to grow had been taken by the weeds. The plants were still alive but were unable to produce much fruit.

This type of soil represents many people who are active in the Church today. They attend their meetings, hold positions in the Church, keep the Word of Wisdom, and pay their tithing, but most of their real effort is directed toward the things of the world. As in the young couple's pitiful garden, the weeds and thorns of the world are sapping their time and energy, and little fruit is being produced. None of us have enough strength to seek riches, pleasures, worldly attention, and spiritual growth. When our desire for fun or money or other worldly things begins to choke our spiritual growth, these things have become weeds that need to be cut back so that we can produce spiritual fruit.

A somewhat humorous example of pleasure becoming a weed happened a few years ago in Salt Lake City. An important meeting had been scheduled for Church leaders where they would be privileged to receive guidance and counsel from one of the General Authorities. That same night an important BYU-Utah basketball game was being carried live on a local television station. Even though most of the leaders showed up at the meeting, many had their hearts set on the game rather than on the counsel they were about to receive. When the person conducting welcomed them there and thanked them for attending the meeting instead of watching the basketball game on television, several men got up and left. They had not realized the game was on television until it was mentioned from the pulpit. Of those who stayed in the meeting, many wore headphones and listened to the game instead of the General Authority. They were physically involved in the Church, but their worldly cares were significantly curtailing their spiritual growth.

The fourth soil mentioned by the Savior was the good ground where the seeds grew and matured and brought forth fruit. This soil represents those who "receive the word in an honest and good heart, having heard the word, keep what they hear, and bring forth fruit with patience" (JST, Luke 8:15).

Marilyn was a young woman who exemplified these attitudes. When she was fifteen years old, her parents gave her permission to be taught the gospel by the missionaries. She was very receptive to the Spirit and was quickly converted to the restored gospel of Jesus Christ. However, because of her age, her parents would not allow her to become a member of the Church. So for two years she faithfully attended the Church and participated in every way she could. She prayed and read the scriptures on a daily basis and continued to grow in testimony and faith. She yearned to be a member of the Church and receive the gift of the Holy Ghost. This was the number-one desire in her life.

As she approached her seventeenth birthday, she met with the current missionaries and asked them to fast with her that she might gain her parents' approval for baptism. Following her special fast, she sat down with her parents and told them how much the Church meant to her and asked that their birthday gift to her be their permission for her to be baptized. They told her that she would have to wait until she was eighteen, but she continued to cry unto the Lord that he would soften the hearts of her parents on her behalf. A few days before her seventeenth birthday, they came to her and told her they had undergone a change of heart, and they gave their permission for her to be baptized. They even gave her their support by coming to the baptism, where they thoroughly enjoyed themselves. Because Marilyn continued to study and learn and live the gospel, the fruits of the Spirit were clearly noticeable in her life. These included the gifts of love, peace, gentleness, goodness, patience, kindness, humility, and joy. These are gifts that all of us can receive as we continue to accept the word of God and nourish it through prayer and obedience. As these spiritual gifts become part of our very nature, we become more like our Father and prepare ourselves for the fullness of joy that exists in the celestial kingdom. We also enjoy life a whole lot more while we're here upon the earth.

15

We Are the Children of God

JOHN 10:1–19

One day a three-year-old wandered away from home. For some reason understood only by three-year-olds, he shed his clothing along the way. Finally he realized he was lost and cold, and he knocked on the door of a nearby house. A young woman answered the door, and, to her surprise, there stood a little boy in his underwear with big tears flowing down his cheeks. She quickly invited him in and wrapped him in a blanket. While she waited for the police to find his mother, she held him on her lap and sang songs to him. They made clown faces in ice cream and drew pictures that he would be able to show his mother. She helped this little lost boy to feel wonderful.

When his mother finally came, he started for the door, but then he stopped and asked, "Are you Heavenly Father's wife?"

This question startled and sobered the young woman. After a few moments of thought, she quietly replied, "No, but I am his daughter." (See Elaine A. Cannon, "Voices," *New Era,* July 1980, p. 16.)

The source of the kindness and sensitivity of this young woman may very well have been her understanding that she truly was a daughter of God—a person of divine parentage. This knowledge can come to us through the Spirit, who will bear witness to us that we are the children of God and joint-heirs with Christ (see Romans 8:16–17). When this knowledge is not just intellectual but has been carried to our hearts by the Spirit, it is accompanied by feelings of joy, confidence, and self-worth. We come to understand that, because we are the children of God, he knows and loves us personally.

We lived with our Father in Heaven for a long time before we came to earth, and he knows us well. He knows our strengths and weaknesses, our likes and dislikes, our needs and wants. Because we do not remember our pre-earthly existence, he knows and understands us much better than we know ourselves. He knows what will be best for us and what experiences we need in order to grow and develop and become like him.

Since we are human and make human mistakes, we sometimes get down on ourselves. Because we compare ourselves with others and can always find someone who seems to live better than we do, we sometimes have a tendency to feel that we are worthless and that God no longer loves us. As we contemplate the billions of people who live on the earth, it is easy to fall into the trap of thinking that we are insignificant to God and that he really doesn't think of us personally, but only as part of a larger group. All these misconceptions are promoted by Satan and are destructive to our spiritual growth and welfare. Discussing our individual importance to God, George Q. Cannon said:

> Now, this is the truth. We humble people, we who feel ourselves sometimes so worthless, so good-for-nothing, we are not so worthless as we think. There is not one of us but what God's love has been expended upon. There is not one of us that He has not cared for and caressed. There is not one of us that He has not desired to save and that He has not devised means to save. There is not one of us that He has not given His angels charge concerning. We may be insignificant and contemptible in our own eyes and in the eyes of others, but the truth remains that we are the children of God and that He has actually given His angels . . . charge concerning us, and they watch over us and have us in their keeping. (*Gospel Truths*, comp. Jerreld L. Newquist, 2 vols. [Salt Lake City: Deseret Book Co., 1974], 1:2.)

Some of the warmest and most comforting verses in all scripture are found in the tenth chapter of John, where Jesus is
described as the good Shepherd. In these verses Jesus assures us
that he calls his sheep by name and that he goes before them and
leads them to pasture. As we decide to respond to the voice of the
Shepherd, we become his sheep. To be led to pasture by the
Savior is one of the greatest promises we could ever receive. It
means that we will receive protection and peace and be nourished
with the true bread of life. We will feel full instead of empty and
feel safe instead of threatened. Our souls will be filled with peace
instead of despair and discouragement because we will know that
the Savior is guiding and protecting us and giving us pasture. The
following story illustrates the great need that all of us have to
know that God is aware of our needs and will give us pasture:

> A grieving young father and his two children sit before a tele-
> vision set in their home after a makeshift dinner. The children have
> been staying with Grandmother while their mother has slowly slipped
> away in a lingering illness; now they and their father are home again
> after her funeral. The little girl drops off to sleep and is carried to her
> bed. The little boy fights off sleepiness until he finally asks his father if
> tonight, just tonight, he can sleep with him in his bed. As the two lie
> silently in the dark, the lad speaks: "Daddy, are you looking at me?"
> "Yes, son," the father replies, "I am looking at you."
>
> The boy sighs and, exhausted, sleeps. The father waits a time
> and then, weeping, cries out in the dark, in anxious anguish: "God,
> are you looking at me? If you are, maybe I can make it. Without
> you, I know I can't." (Marion D. Hanks, "Changing Channels,"
> *Ensign*, November 1990, p. 39.)

In the tenth chapter of John, Jesus assures this grieving father
and all of us that he knows and cares for each of his sheep. Saying
that he is not like a hireling who "careth not for the sheep," he
declares, "I am the good shepherd, and know my sheep . . . and I
lay down my life for the sheep." (John 10:13–15.) He explains

that his objective for us is "that they might have life, and that they might have it more abundantly" (v. 10).

The great concern that God has for each of us, even when we are not responding to his gospel, is demonstrated numerous times every day all over the world. Here is just one example.

Elder James M. Paramore was assigned to conduct a stake conference in New Mexico. Usually he would fly to Albuquerque, rent a car, and drive to the conference in Grants. However, Elder Paramore felt impressed that he should fly to Gallup and get a car there. This meant flying in a tiny plane in which he was the only passenger. It was an extremely windy day, and there were times during the plane ride that he wondered if they would land safely.

When he tried to rent a car at the airport, it was discovered that his driver's license had expired a week earlier. When he called the local bishop to see if the bishop could pick him up, he caught him just going out the door to perform a marriage. The bishop said that he would try to arrange a ride for him. "We don't have a conference here today," he said. "What are you doing in Gallup?"

The bishop's question demonstrated how far out of the way the Lord had guided Elder Paramore for purposes only the Lord was aware of. About this time a man dressed in work clothes stepped forward and said: "I understand you are in a little trouble. I just came by to get some applications to take flying lessons, and I couldn't help hearing that you need help. Could I take you somewhere?"

After listening to Elder Paramore's dilemma, the man volunteered to drive him if he would pay for the gas. They climbed into the man's old, worn-out car and started the sixty-mile drive to Grants, New Mexico. Elder Paramore decided to do some missionary work and asked the man several questions, such as: "What do you know about the Mormons?" "Have you ever been to Salt Lake City?" "Have you ever read the Book of Mormon?" When Elder Paramore asked the man if he knew the Book of Mormon was true, there was a long pause and the man said:

I'm an elder in the Church, and two years ago my wife left me and my two children for another man. I was a member of the branch presidency where I live. The members of my branch cut me off and blamed me for the departure of my wife. We've never been able to go back to church because of those feelings.

Do I know if the Book of Mormon is true, Brother Paramore? (I knew who you were.) I've read the Book of Mormon many times, and I know it's as true as anything on this earth.

During the next hour and a half, Elder Paramore came to realize that he was sitting in the presence of a great man who had been deeply hurt and was struggling spiritually. They discussed many wonderful things, including the hope of the man's son someday serving a mission. Later Elder Paramore wrote him weekly, and he began making great progress. Elder Paramore concluded this story with the following testimony:

Now, think about it. There are five billion people upon the earth, and here was one man out in the wilderness about whom the Lord was concerned. So he sent a General Authority, all unknowing, out of his way, redirecting his path. It could have been anyone, but it happened to be me. And when I came home that day, I knew that God loves all his children. ("Leadership—Jesus Was the Perfect Leader," *Brigham Young University 1989–90 Devotional and Fireside Speeches* [Provo: Brigham Young University Press, 1990], pp. 3–4.)

When our Heavenly Father sent us down to this earth to work out our exaltation, he did not leave us alone. He gave us the Savior and his great atonement so that we could have the chance to return to him. He gave us the scriptures to guide us and help us make correct decisions throughout our lives. We have living prophets and apostles to help us better understand the scriptures and apply the word of God as we face today's problems and challenges. We also have the gift of the Holy Ghost, which brings us great comfort, peace, and guidance as we strive to do the will of our Father. One of the greatest gifts that he has given us is the opportunity to communicate with him each day in holy, sacred prayer. He has told us that we can pray to him silently as well as vocally and discuss with him our temporal as well as spiritual and emotional needs.

Because we are his children, our Heavenly Father loves each one of us and desires to help each of us become as he is. The realization that we are loved of God is the very basis of our relationship with him. As this truth sinks deep within our hearts, we develop the faith and confidence in God that we need in order to place our lives in his hands. Turning our lives over to God always brings deep satisfaction and peace, for we come to know that we are on the path to eternal life.

16

The Parable of the Tares

MATTHEW 13:24–43

I recently heard a story that effectively teaches an important gospel principle. Since no reference is available, the story may or may not be true, but this does not affect the value of its message.

Just before boarding a plane, a woman stopped at one of the airport shops and purchased a magazine and a bag of cookies. After the plane had taken off, she undid her seat belt and made herself as comfortable as possible. She picked up the magazine lying next to her cookies on the tray in front of her and began to read. About this time the man next to her reached over, ripped open her bag of cookies, and offered her one. He then took one for himself. Much to her surprise, he took a second cookie—then a third one. Afraid that none would be left for her, she quickly began to eat the cookies. They took turns eating the cookies until there was just one left. To her astonishment and outrage, the stranger picked up the last cookie and broke it in half. He then gave one half to her and ate the other half himself. She felt so indignant at his brazenness that she refused to talk to him even though he attempted several times to involve her in a friendly conversation.

She sighed in relief when the plane finally landed and she no longer had to sit next to a person who had shown such arrogance and rudeness. After entering the terminal, she reached into her travel bag for her purse and there, to her surprise and chagrin, was her package of cookies—still unopened. Evidently the man had also purchased a bag of cookies and had been sharing his bag with her. Instead of him being the rude one, she had eaten his cookies as fast as he did, failed to thank him, and refused to speak with him. She quickly looked around to try and make things right, but it was too late—he was nowhere to be seen.

This story demonstrates one of the reasons Jesus warned us against unrighteous judgment and told us to judge righteously (see JST, Matthew 7:1). It is so easy to judge incorrectly. Because we do not know the motives of others and because appearances and circumstances can be deceiving, we need the help of the Holy Ghost in order to judge righteously. The Lord said, "Put your trust in that Spirit which leadeth to do good—yea, to do justly, to walk humbly, *to judge righteously;* and this is my Spirit" (D&C 11:12; emphasis added).

A positive attitude toward others can also help us exercise righteous judgment. The great difference that attitude can make was illustrated by a young couple who had been married for two years. One day the wife ran across a magazine article that suggested married couples schedule regular discussions so each of them could frankly and forthrightly identify the habits and idiosyncrasies they found irritating in the other.

Since the wife was annoyed by many things that her husband did, she felt this was a great idea. Even though the husband was hesitant, after the wife coaxed him a little he finally agreed to give it a try. Each of them were to name five things that they found annoying, and the wife volunteered to go first.

In describing this event more than fifty years later, this the wife remembered only the first item on her list: she didn't like the way her husband ate grapefruit, peeling it and eating it like an orange. The other items, she recalled, were probably similar.

Then it was her husband's turn. Concerning what happened next, she wrote:

> Though it has been more than half a century, I still carry a mental image of my husband's handsome young face as he gathered his brows together in a thoughtful, puzzled frown and then looked at

me with his large blue-gray eyes and said, "Well, to tell the truth, I can't think of anything I don't like about you, Honey."

Gasp.

I quickly turned my back, because I didn't know how to explain the tears that had filled my eyes and were running down my face. I had found fault with him over such trivial things as the way he ate grapefruit, while he hadn't even noticed any of my peculiar and no doubt annoying ways. (Lola B. Walters, "The Grapefruit Syndrome," *Ensign,* April 1993, p. 13.)

Too many times we spend our time looking for the bad instead of the good. Here was a good marriage that has now lasted over fifty years, and yet the young wife was getting hung up on how her husband ate grapefruit. Our relationships are too important to allow insignificant or unrighteous judgment to damage or derail them.

Sometimes a judgmental attitude can seriously affect our service in the Church. President Gordon B. Hinckley found that just changing our basic attitude toward others can cause great growth in individuals and their service to the Lord.

For a number of years, while I had responsibility for the work in Asia, I interviewed each missionary one-on-one. I asked each what virtue he or she saw in his or her companion. . . .

When I raised that question, almost invariably the missionary, an elder for example, would stop with a surprised look on his face. He had never thought of his companion that way before. He had seen his faults and weaknesses but had not seen his virtues. I would tell him to pause and think about it for a minute. Then the answers would begin to come. Such answers as, "He's a hard worker." "He gets up in the morning." "He dresses neatly." "He doesn't complain."

It was a remarkable thing, really. These young men and women, for the most part, had been oblivious to the virtues of their companions, although they were well aware of their companions' faults, and often felt discouraged because of them. But when they began to turn their attitudes around, remarkable things began to happen. ("Strengthening Each Other," *Ensign,* February 1985, pp. 3–4.)

One of the most damaging consequences of judging unrighteously is the negative effect it can have on the soul-growth of those being judged. The Savior warned us of this serious problem in the parable of the tares. He likened the kingdom of heaven to a man who sowed good seed in his field. During the night, the enemy came and sowed tares among the wheat. In this case the tares could very well have been darnel, a weedy grass that looks like wheat until the wheat matures and begins to bring forth fruit. When the servants asked if they should go and pull up the tares from among the wheat, the master said, "Nay; lest while ye gather up the tares, ye root up also the wheat with them. Let both grow together until the harvest: and in the time of harvest I will say to the reapers, Gather ye together first the tares, and bind them in bundles to burn them: but gather the wheat into my barn." (See Matthew 13:24–30.)

If the workers tried to remove the tares from the wheat too early, they would also uproot part of the wheat. They were to wait until the roots of the wheat were strong and fully developed so that the wheat would not be ripped out with the tares. Also, until the wheat was fully mature, some of it could have been falsely perceived as tares and destroyed.

One of the important messages of this parable is that God is giving everyone an opportunity to fully mature and develop into either wheat or tares. If we are not careful, we will try to judge and separate people too soon—people who look and even act like tares but who with love and patience might mature into wheat and become fruitful. This transformation from apparent tare to fruitful wheat is constantly occurring in God's earthly kingdom.

A few years ago two girls walked into a seminary class. To most people they looked very much like tares. One of them had shaved half her head and painted it black and dyed the hair left on the other half fluorescent orange. The second girl had done the same thing except that instead of fluorescent orange she had dyed her hair green with white bleach streaks. They both wore wild clothing and several sets of earrings in each ear. The teacher found himself having a hard time reserving judgment on them and knew the students in the class would have a difficult time also. Several days later, when the two girls were absent, the teacher asked the class members to overlook the outward appearance of the girls and show love to them. He asked them to accept the girls as friends.

Around Thanksgiving the seminary class held a testimony meeting and, to the amazement of the teacher, the two girls were in attendance. Near the end of the meeting one of the girls walked to the front of the classroom and said: "At school I am laughed at, my parents hassle me, and everywhere I go people make fun of me. Seminary is the only place I feel love. I know my teacher loves me, and I know my class loves me. I have never been made fun of or laughed at in seminary. I'm not accepted anywhere else but here. I don't have a testimony, but I think I'm getting one and I think the gospel is true."

By the end of the year a "metamorphosis as real as a cocoon turning into a butterfly had taken place." As love and acceptance literally changed the girls' lives, their spiritual growth was accompanied by a change in their physical appearance. Because these two girls were not discarded as tares and were given the opportunity to grow, they became fruitful daughters of our Father in Heaven. (See CES Teleconference Packet, 24 June 1989.)

Habitual criticism and a tendency to judge unrighteously may suggest underlying problems of pride or exaggerated self-worth. The unknown author of the following poem addressed this problem in a humorous way:

> I dreamed that death came the other night
> And heaven's gate swung wide.
> With kindly grace an angel
> Ushered me inside.
>
> And there to my astonishment
> Stood folks I'd known on earth.
> Some I'd judged and labeled
> As "unfit" or of "little worth."

Indignant words rose to my lips
But never were set free.
For on every face showed stunned surprise—
No one expected me!

Acceptance of others comes more easily to those who perceive that they have spiritual and physical flaws of their own. Humility brings the Spirit, and the Spirit helps us judge righteously. As we begin to feel better about others, we find that we feel better about ourselves and enjoy life more. Greater peace and happiness come to those who find the good in others and do what they can to help them fulfill their divine potential.

17

Help Thou Mine Unbelief

MARK 9:14–29

One day the Savior was approached by a distressed father whose son had been possessed with an evil spirit from the time he was a child. The spirit would dash him on the ground and cause him to foam at the mouth and gnash his teeth, and it had on many occasions cast him into fire or into water to destroy him. The father asked Jesus to have compassion on them and cast the evil spirit out of his son.

Jesus said unto the father, "If thou canst believe, all things are possible to him that believeth" (Mark 9:23). The father's reply revealed an honest and sincere heart. He cried out and said with tears, "Lord, I believe; help thou mine unbelief" (v. 24).

Jesus then rebuked the evil spirit and commanded him to come out of the son, which left the son lying on the ground as though he was dead. In fact, many of the people in the crowd stated that he was dead. But Jesus took the young man's hand and "lifted him up; and he arose." (See Mark 9:24–27.)

This man's simple and heartfelt statement, "I believe; help thou mine unbelief," may be one of the most significant statements in all scripture. This guileless, unpretentious declaration reveals a heart filled with humility, faith, and an overwhelming desire to qualify for the blessings of the Lord. The father knew he had faith, yet he was afraid that his faith was not strong enough to bless his son. He reached out to Jesus for help and support so that his faith might increase.

Many who are less active or struggling with sin may be like this father. They have faith, but they need some assistance in order to increase their faith and receive the help and blessings of the Lord. This was the case with a man named Michael. In the following story he shares how others helped him increase his faith so that he could receive the strength to be spiritually healed of the Lord:

> My marriage had failed. I was living a life contrary to the prin-
> ciples of the Church. Not only was I inactive but had lost confi-
> dence in my ability to go back. I became successful in business,
> drove the nicest car, and bought expensive clothes. I had everything
> that the world would want.
>
> One day, my company hired Ken Wheeler, whom I knew to be
> a Mormon by the way he acted. We became friends, and he invited
> me to Church. I wanted to go but didn't feel worthy. He continued
> to invite me, and I continued to refuse. I wanted to get back, but I
> didn't have the strength to do it.
>
> One night, alone in my apartment, I became very depressed and
> broke into uncontrollable sobs. I prayed to the Lord and begged for
> His help. The next day Ken asked me how I was doing; he could
> sense something was wrong. Putting his arms around me, he said,
> "He still loves you, and we do, too. Why don't you come back
> home?" That was the answer to my prayers; that was the help I had
> begged for the night before.
>
> I came home! I felt uncomfortable at first, but the feeling that
> everyone cared made it easier. Today, I don't drive the nicest car or
> wear the fanciest clothes, but I feel richer than ever. (Quoted in David
> B. Haight, "People to People," *Ensign*, November 1981, p. 60.)

Sometimes we desire to help others increase their faith but feel that we don't have the opportunity or the know-how. This just is not true. The Lord has organized his Church in such a way that all of us have the opportunity to help others simply through our normal Church service. For example, two Relief Society sisters visited a particular home and shared their love and testimonies, just as numerous sisters do all over the world. They had no idea of the impact their visit would have on this family but were just trying to fulfill their responsibilities.

About a year later, while the husband of one of the sisters was teaching some priesthood brethren about the importance of visiting their assigned families, a thirty-five-year-old man told him of his wife's visit the year before. Then he said: "May I tell you a secret? My entire family had decided the day before your wife came to visit that we were leaving the Church, offended, never to return. I bear witness to you that we felt the Lord speak through her as she stirred us up in remembrance of God and our ordinances. I'm a member of a bishopric now. I would not be here today if it were not for her." (Quoted in Gene R. Cook, "Inviting Others to 'Come unto Christ,'" *Ensign,* November 1988, p. 39.)

This family possessed some faith, but their faith was not strong enough to withstand the offense they had received. Through fulfilling a normal Church assignment, these two sisters helped the family increase their faith and overcome this difficulty. After he became a member of a bishopric, this man was in a position to help others increase their faith through his faithful service in his calling.

This same principle was demonstrated by a dedicated home teacher who received the following letter from a Latter-day Saint girl who belonged to a less-active family.

> You were the bright hope in my often difficult life. There is no greater call than a home teacher. You loved and showed respect for my parents. You honored them and at the same time supported me. *You were there!* . . . As I look back now, I realize you and the truth you offered were my life-support.
>
> Behind the doors were years of pain, tears, and fear. You were able to come into our home and chase them away, if only for a short time. No one else could do that. (Quoted in Dallin H. Oaks, "Modern Pioneers," *Ensign,* November 1989, p. 67; emphasis in original.)

As we strengthen and assist others, we assist ourselves as well. As we bear testimony, our testimonies grow. When we teach the gospel to others, our own gospel understanding increases. As we give service and charity to those who need help, we become more charitable and our peace and happiness increase.

Robert was a college student who knew the Church was true but had lost his enthusiasm for the gospel. His thoughts were centered on his career, and he felt that pure, Christlike living was not really possible. Going to church had become a ritual, and the gospel was not a deep source of fulfillment to him.

One day he came to realize that his problem was that he was not living up to what he knew was true. He started to put more effort into his Church service and into his personal gospel study, but still he felt little spiritual growth. Then an announcement was made in priesthood meeting that led to a dramatic change in his life. The priesthood brethren were asked to assist a couple who were moving. Robert usually ignored such announcements, but this time he made the decision to help.

When the designated day arrived, it was hot and muggy. Robert had a heavy school schedule and many other things to do, but he was determined to follow through on his commitment to help. As he approached the house, he felt apprehensive and embarrassed. After he saw the countless boxes that needed to be loaded on the truck, he decided he would help for an hour and then leave.

As he started carrying boxes out to the truck, "a small miracle happened" and he began to enjoy himself. Robert explains what happened next:

> I "lost myself" in giving and wound up staying the whole after-noon—until the entire truck was packed.
>
> I rode home feeling sweaty and wonderful.
>
> At four the next morning, I awoke with butterflies in my stomach. Why was I so excited? Because I had done something I didn't have to do. And it felt good!

> "I wish I could feel that way all the time," I thought. . . . I got
> up, knelt, and poured out my heart to my Heavenly Father. I felt a
> warmth come over me, and my tears flowed freely. At last I was tast-
> ing the fruits of my efforts to better live the gospel. (Robert K. Rey,
> "I'll Stay for an Hour," *Ensign*, February 1989, p. 63.)

Robert may not have been the only person who spiritually
benefited from his help. It's reasonable to assume that the family's
feelings of faith, love, and appreciation increased as well. At least
this is what happened to our family when we recently received
help from ward members in a move that we needed to make.

No matter what our circumstances are, we can build up and
help others. I watched my mother, who was bedridden for ten
years, reach out to others every day of her life. She would knit
gifts for people and write letters of encouragement to those who
were down. She taught a Primary class from her bed in the living
room, and those who came to comfort her left inspired by their
visit. She contacted community centers to see what needs they
had that she could fulfill from her bed. Each day she would
receive a list of people to call who were bedridden and lonely.
Calling from her own bed, she would cheer them up and replace
their despair with hope. As my mother learned to build up and
serve others, her own situation became more bearable and the
Holy Ghost brought peace and happiness into her life. Because of
her willing service and desire to live the gospel, she received the
companionship of the Holy Ghost and her own life was enriched.
All of us will enjoy life more as we strive to assist others in the
challenges they face.

18

If Ye Loved Me, Ye Would Rejoice

JOHN 14:28

When hundreds of people were recently asked what they feared most, the answer a majority of them gave was death. Most of them did not fear the actual act of dying as much as not knowing what conditions will exist after they die. This response is not surprising, since much of the world knows little about life after death.

Because of this lack of information, the loss of a loved one leaves many people empty and seemingly comfortless. Their separation is considered permanent, and their hearts are filled with sorrow and distress. This is not the way God intended it to be.

On the eve of his crucifixion, Jesus met with his Apostles and ate the last Passover meal with them. He introduced the sacrament and washed the feet of the Twelve. Jesus taught his disciples the importance of loving one another, spoke of his many mansions in heaven, and promised them the power of the Holy Ghost.

Jesus then taught them a great principle concerning death: "Ye have heard how I said unto you, I go away, and come again unto you. If ye loved me, ye would *rejoice,* because I said, I go unto the Father: for my Father is greater than I." (John 14:28; emphasis added.)

Jesus is suggesting that as we come to understand his wonderful atonement and other gospel principles concerning life after death, we will feel happy for those loved ones who pass away. This does not mean that we will not feel sorrow or loneliness, for God has told us that we should "weep for the loss of them that die" (D&C 42:45). What it does mean is that we will understand the great blessings that they are participating in and feel good for them even though we miss them. We realize that as one of us passes away here, there are numerous loved ones on the other side of the veil who participate in a joyous reunion.

My own father, at this writing, died just a few months ago, and his family and friends consider it a wonderful blessing. He was suffering from several painful physical ailments at the time of his death. Because of our understanding of the gospel, we realize that he is now in a better place, and, as Jesus said, we rejoice for him. We miss our association with him but appreciate the blessings he is now receiving. These kinds of feelings are beautifully illustrated by an incident related by President Thomas S. Monson. While he was attending the viewing for a wife and mother who had died young, the smallest child in the family expressed to him her certainty that her family would all be together again one day. Concerning this incident, President Monson concluded: "Sustained by her unfailing testimony, knowing that life continues beyond the grave, she, her father, her brothers, her sisters, and indeed all who share this knowledge of divine truth can declare to the world: 'Weeping may endure for a night, but joy cometh in the morning.' (Ps. 30:5.)" ("Hopeless Dawn—Joyful Morning," *Ensign,* February 1993, p. 5.)

President Joseph F. Smith's father, Hyrum, was martyred when Joseph F. was but five years old. He was only thirteen when his mother became ill and passed away. In spite of the hardship this brought upon him and his family, his faith in the wonderful atonement of Christ led him to testify of the joyful reunion that awaited him: "I cannot express the joy I feel at the thought of meeting my father, and my precious mother, who gave me birth in the midst of persecution and poverty. . . . The thought of meeting her, who can express the joy? The thought of meeting my children who have preceded me beyond the veil, and of meeting my kindred and my friends, what happiness it affords! For I know that I shall meet them there. God has shown me that this is true. He has made it clear to me, in answer to my prayer and devotion, as he has made it clear to the understanding of all men who have sought diligently to know him." (*Gospel Doctrine*, 5th ed. [Salt Lake City: Deseret Book Co., 1939], p. 429.)

It is apparent that Joseph F. Smith did not fear death but looked upon it as a future blessing that would reunite him with his loved ones. President Spencer W. Kimball taught that when we say that early death is a calamity or a tragedy, we are saying that mortality is preferable to early entrance into the spirit world and to eventual salvation and exaltation. He said that the gospel teaches us that there is no tragedy in death but only in sin. (See *Tragedy or Destiny,* Brigham Young University Speeches of the Year [Provo, 6 December 1955], p. 2.) Joseph Smith declared that "the only difference between the old and young dying is, one lives longer in heaven and eternal light and glory than the other, and is freed a little sooner from this miserable, wicked world" (*History of the Church* 4:554).

Sometimes, because of our love for them, we beg the Lord to allow people to live who might be much better off on the other side of the veil. As we come to understand that no one really dies but just moves on to a new environment and different responsibilities, it becomes easier to place our trust in the Lord and ask that his will be done. This usually makes it much better for both the person who is sick and his or her loved ones.

An understanding of the gospel can help us face our own death with courage and peace. This was superbly illustrated by a teenager named Greg who suffered from bone cancer. At first he lost one of his legs, but the cancer continued to spread until his lungs were infected with the disease. He was told that he had only a few months to live. When a family conversation bogged down in grief and dejection, he said: "I can't go on like this. I have to go on planning to live. There is always time for dying, but there isn't always time for living." Through his fear and pain he quietly went about living his life and doing the best he could do.

Shortly before his death, Greg dictated the following final entry for his journal:

> Life has been good to me. Although I have had many disappointments, I have had many, many satisfactions. . . . Saturday, August 1, my soul was wrought up. It was extremely difficult for me to get a breath, and I hurt every time I tried. Now a feeling of peace has come over me. . . . My prayers have been answered many times, and I am grateful to the Lord for his many blessings. Somehow, the mere physical sports, which I valued so highly before, seem as nothing compared to the tasks that I will soon embark upon. I bid the reader farewell, wishing the Lord's blessings upon him. I have no feeling of bitterness, no malice of any kind, for I know in my heart that this is the Lord's will. I know truly that the Lord does live. And I know that only through obeying his commandments can we be happy on earth. (Quoted in Jean Hart, "I Knew Courage," *Improvement Era*, April 1970, p. 40.)

As we make the atonement of Jesus part of our lives, we too can overcome the fear of death and look forward to a wonderful reunion in the next life. The powerful effect the Atonement can have was demonstrated well by the converted Lamanites who became known as the people of Ammon. They were willing to lay down on the ground and allow their Lamanite brethren to kill them rather than pick up the sword and break a vow they had made with the Lord. The Book of Mormon states that "they never did look upon death with any degree of terror, for their hope and views of Christ and the resurrection; therefore, death was swallowed up to them by the victory of Christ over it" (Alma 27:28).

Just as birth into this life was a farewell from our previous one, death in this life is but an entrance into a better one. Because of the atonement of Jesus Christ, death is just another essential step in Heavenly Father's plan for us. God has promised us and our loved ones that when we live the gospel and endure to the end, death will be sweet unto us (see D&C 42:46).

19

Obtaining Growth and Peace Through the Sacrament

JST, MATTHEW 26:22–25

The last night Jesus spent in mortality was one of the most important nights in all of history. This is the night that he suffered for our sins in the Garden of Gethsemane. It is also the night that he introduced the sacrament to his Apostles after partaking of the last Passover meal with them. This meal is often referred to as the Last Supper, and it marked the end of looking forward to the Savior's infinite sacrifice through the offering of lambs on the altar. He replaced this ordinance of sacrifice with the sacramental ordinance, which has the purpose of focusing our minds and hearts on the extraordinary gift of his atonement. Matthew recorded the introduction of this sacred ordinance:

> And as they were eating, Jesus took bread and brake it, and blessed it, and gave to his disciples, and said, Take, eat; this is in remembrance of my body which I give a ransom for you.
>
> And he took the cup, and gave thanks, and gave it to them, saying, Drink ye all of it.
>
> For this is in remembrance of my blood of the new testament, which is shed for as many as shall believe on my name, for the remission of their sins.
>
> And I give unto you a commandment, that ye shall observe to do the things which ye have seen me do, and bear record of me even unto the end. (JST, Matthew 26:22–25.)

Because we have an opportunity to partake of the sacrament almost every week of the year, many have become complacent concerning this ordinance and fail to realize the importance it plays in our quest for peace here and eternal life in the world to come. If we live to be in our seventies, we will renew this sacramental covenant well over 3,000 times. The frequency of the sacrament does not lessen its importance but actually suggests that it must be of vital importance in God's plan.

President Joseph Fielding Smith emphasized the importance of the sacrament: "No member of the Church can fail to make this covenant [the sacrament] and renew it week by week, and retain the Spirit of the Lord. The Sacrament meeting of the Church is the most important meeting which we have. . . . Those who persist in their absence from this service will eventually lose the Spirit." (*Church History and Modern Revelation* [Salt Lake City: Quorum of the Twelve Apostles of The Church of Jesus Christ of Latter-day Saints, 1946], p. 123.)

The Doctrine and Covenants states that "in the ordinances thereof, the power of godliness is manifest" (84:20). The ordinances, including the sacrament, are channels of power through which we can literally partake of the Spirit and power of God. Our ability to live the gospel and have a personal relationship with Christ can be greatly strengthened through worthy participation in the sacrament.

Not just participation but worthy participation is required in order to receive the blessings God desires to give us. Elder John H. Groberg explained what it means to partake of the sacrament worthily.

What does it mean to partake of the sacrament worthily? Or how do we know if we are unworthy?

If we desire to improve (which is to repent) and are not under priesthood restriction, then, in my opinion, we are worthy. If, however, we have no desire to improve, if we have no intention of following the guidance of the Spirit, we must ask: Are we worthy to partake, or are we making a mockery of the very purpose of the sacrament, which is to act as a catalyst for personal repentance and improvement? ("The Beauty and Importance of the Sacrament," *Ensign,* May 1989, p. 38.)

Elder Groberg's insightful comment that one of the main purposes of the sacrament is to act as a catalyst for personal repentance and improvement gives us guidance concerning what we can do during the sacrament to make this ordinance more meaningful in our lives. Not only should we contemplate Jesus and his suffering, death, and resurrection in our behalf, but we also should ponder our own lives and what we need to do in order to become more like him. As we analyze our own lives with a prayerful heart, the Spirit will sometimes indicate areas of our lives that need to be strengthened. By committing to work on these areas and asking the Lord to help us, we can gain real strength and power through the sacramental ordinance. Greater peace and happiness will accompany this growth process.

When we partake of the sacrament, we renew all of the covenants we have made with the Lord and make three very important promises. We witness that we are willing to take upon us the name of Christ, that we will always remember him, and that we will keep all of his commandments. We give God our word that we will do the very best we can do to keep these promises. In return, he promises that we will have his Spirit to be with us. His Spirit is the source of great joy, peace, power, understanding, and guidance. To receive the heavenly gift of the Spirit is vital in our quest for peace, happiness, and eternal life.

Elder David O. McKay explained these three promises as follows:

> The first: That we are willing to take upon ourselves the name of the Son. In so doing we choose him as our leader and our ideal; and he is the one perfect character in all the world. It is a glorious thing to be a member of the Church of Christ and to be called a Christian in the true sense of the term; and we promise that we should like to be that, that we are willing to do it.

Secondly, that we will always remember him. Not just on Sunday, but on Monday, in our daily acts, in our self-control. When our brother hurts us we are going to try to master our feelings and not retaliate in the same spirit of anger. When a brother treats us with contempt we are going to try to return kindness. That's the spirit of the Christ and that's what we have promised—that we will do our best to achieve these high standards of Christianity, true Christian principles.

The third: We promise to "keep the commandments which he has given." Tithing, fast offerings, the Word of Wisdom, kindness, forgiveness, love. The obligation of a member of the Church of Christ is great, but it is as glorious as it is great, because obedience to these principles gives life, eternal life. (In Conference Report, October 1929, p. 14.)

As members of the Savior's church, we represent him to the rest of the world. President Gordon B. Hinckley reminded us that "as his followers, we cannot do a mean or shoddy or ungracious thing without tarnishing his image. Nor can we do a good and gracious and generous act without burnishing more brightly the symbol of him whose name we have taken upon ourselves." (*Be Thou an Example* [Salt Lake City: Deseret Book Co., 1981], p. 90.)

The blessings of the sacrament require a total commitment to the Lord and his will. The Lord expects us to commit to keep *all* of his commandments, not just most of them. Nephi saw our day and indicated that many would say that "he will justify in committing a *little* sin; yea, lie a *little,* take the advantage of one because of his words, dig a pit for thy neighbor; there is no harm in this; . . . if it so be that we are guilty, God will beat us with a *few* stripes, and at last we shall be saved in the kingdom of God" (2 Nephi 28:8; emphasis added).

Nephi goes on to say that these teachings are "false and vain and foolish doctrines" (v. 9). The problem Nephi describes is one of commitment. Many are willing to do some things and even most things that God desires but hold back from making a complete commitment to the Lord. The Lord has indicated over and over again that he requires *all* our heart, might, mind, and strength, not just part of it (see Moroni 10:32; D&C 4, 20:31).

This lack of total commitment was illustrated in a survey that was done among Latter-day Saint seminary students. Hundreds of students were asked to respond to fifteen actions that have been forbidden by the Lord by marking each one "Always okay," "Usually okay," "Occasionally okay," or "Never okay." The big numbers showed up in the "Occasionally okay" column. Nearly every student felt it was occasionally okay to watch R-rated movies, steady date, use the Lord's name in vain, read pornographic magazines, tell crude jokes, and break other commandments God has given us. As we analyze this attitude, it becomes apparent that most of these students have not committed to obey *all* of the Lord's commandments or to keep his commandments *all* of the time. If we feel it is okay to break most of God's commandments some of the time, we will always be breaking some of his commandments.

This same attitude has surfaced in an activity one teacher uses in his classes. He will ask the students to record on a piece of paper their answers to three simple questions. The first question is, "Do you feel that God loves all of us children?" Nearly every student writes down a yes answer to this question. The second question is, "Since God loves us, will he ever ask us to do anything that is not for our own good?" Nearly all the students respond to this question with a no. The third question is, "Since God loves us and will never ask us to do anything that is not for our good, are you willing to do anything he asks you to do?" Over the years very few students have been willing to answer yes to this question. To make a commitment to do whatever God wants them to do is beyond their faith and trust in God. They want to hear each separate request of God and decide on each one individually.

Yet this is the very commitment that is necessary if we desire to receive the blessings of the sacrament. We need to be willing to commit to try to live all of God's commandments. There is no greater reward than that of being at peace in a world of turmoil. President Spencer W. Kimball indicated that "such peace comes only through integrity. When we make a covenant or agreement with God, we must keep it at whatever cost." ("The Example of Abraham," *Ensign,* June 1975, p. 6.)

President Ezra Taft Benson identified ten blessings that come as we truly turn our lives over to the Savior. "Men and women who turn their lives over to God will find out that he can make a lot more out of their lives than they can. He will deepen their joys, expand their vision, quicken their minds, strengthen their muscles, lift their spirits, multiply their blessings, increase their opportunities, comfort their souls, raise up friends, and pour out peace. Whoever will lose his life to God will find he has eternal life." ("Jesus Christ—Gifts and Expectations," *New Era,* May 1975, p. 20.)

As we participate in the sacrament each week focused on the purpose of the ordinance, sincere about improving our lives, and appreciative of the marvelous atonement of the Savior, a feeling of power and peace will permeate our souls. We will enjoy the peace that comes from being one with God and feel the power he gives those who commit to him. This power will enable us to overcome the world and become more like him. It will strengthen our ability to conquer attitudes and behaviors that are keeping us from the peace and happiness we desire. This power will "wrought a mighty change in us, or in our hearts, that we have no more disposition to do evil, but to do good continually" (Mosiah 5:2).

20

Messages from the Cross
MATTHEW 27, LUKE 23, JOHN 19

All of us are well aware of the humiliation, persecution, pain, and suffering that accompanied the last twenty-four hours of the Savior's earthly ministry. The depth of his pain for our sins in the Garden of Gethsemane is impossible for us to comprehend. That trial was immediately followed by the betrayal of Judas, one of his close apostles and friends. What was left of the night was spent in abuse and humiliation as Jewish leaders led him through several mock trials. When morning came Jesus was accused and condemned before Pilate, scourged by the Roman soldiers, and taken to the hill Golgotha to be crucified. Unfeeling soldiers drove spikes into his hands, wrists, and feet, and he was left on the cross to die. Death by crucifixion was used by the Romans because it caused enormous physical pain and suffering.

What is incredible is that in the midst of this exhaustion and pain, Jesus continued to reach out to others who needed comfort and peace. Perhaps his greatest sermon was taught in the seven short statements that he uttered from the cross, for they reveal the very heart and soul of the Savior.

His first statement demonstrated his concern for the soldiers who had just nailed him to the cross. While many of them were in the process of ridiculing and mocking him, he said, "Father, forgive them; for they know not what they do" (Luke 23:34).

Some have felt that he was forgiving them of their sins as he had forgiven others during his ministry, but this was not the case.

Such forgiveness requires repentance and baptism. Elder Bruce R. McConkie explained that, in effect, Jesus was saying: "Father lay not this sin to their charge [the sin of nailing him to the cross], for they are acting under orders, and those upon whom the full and real guilt rests are their rulers and the Jewish conspirators who caused me to be condemned. It is Caiaphas and Pilate who know I am innocent; these soldiers are just carrying out their orders." (*Doctrinal New Testament Commentary,* 3 vols. [Salt Lake City: Bookcraft, 1965–73], 1:818–19.)

On the cross Jesus put into practice his command to "bless them that curse you, do good to them that hate you, and pray for them which despitefully use you, and persecute you" (Matthew 5:44). Right to the end he showed us the way that we must live if we desire to return to our Father.

The source of much of the misery and heartache that exists in the world today is the destructive spirit of hate, revenge, and lack of forgiveness that permeates the hearts of many. God wants us to forgive every offense so we can enjoy peace and happiness and continue to feel the promptings of his Spirit.

The utter waste that the refusal to forgive can bring was described by an elderly man at his brother's funeral. The two brothers had lived together in a small, one-room cabin from the time they were young men. Following a quarrel they had divided the room in half with a chalk line, and for *sixty-two years* they had neither crossed the line nor spoken a word to one another. Now one brother was dead, and the other brother felt deep sorrow for the years together they had lost. (See Thomas S. Monson, "Mercy—The Divine Gift," *Ensign,* May 1995, p. 59.)

In marvelous contrast to this experience is the story of Paul Hulme, who had much more to overcome than a quarrel with a loved one. His ten-year-old daughter, Kelly, had been raped and killed by a teenage boy. To have his youngest child so brutally attacked brought deep feelings of anger and bitterness.

As he turned to the Lord, Paul came to understand that his daughter was in a place where people loved her and that he needed to resolve his own bitterness before it destroyed his future spiritual well-being. The Spirit guided his thoughts to the family of the teenager who had killed his daughter, and he began to understand how they must feel. He visited the family and endeavored to comfort and help them.

Bishop Hulme never knew whether or not his visit helped the family, but he recognized the great impact it had on his own life. Through his efforts to forgive and help, a miracle occurred in his own heart and his hate and bitterness were replaced with charity. His future life was forever different because he was willing to forgive. (See Roderick J. Linton, "The Forgiving Heart," *Ensign*, April 1993, pp. 15–16.)

The next statement Jesus made was to one of the thieves hanging on a cross next to him. In answer to the request, "Lord, remember me when thou comest into thy kingdom," the Savior replied, "Verily I say unto thee, To day shalt thou be with me in paradise" (Luke 23:42–43).

A better translation would have been, "This day thou shalt be with me in the *world of spirits*" (see Joseph Smith, *Teachings of the Prophet Joseph Smith*, comp. Joseph Fielding Smith [Salt Lake City: Deseret Book Co., 1977], p. 309; emphasis added). Jesus was not suggesting that the man was forgiven, but, recognizing the seeds of faith and repentance and realizing the possibility of conversion and progress in the spirit world, he desired to offer hope to the thief.

In just a few hours Jesus was going to meet with the righteous spirits in the spirit world and organize them so that the gospel could be offered to those who would have believed if the truth had been offered to them in this life. The thief may very well be one of these.

Righteous spirits who have been converted to the gospel in spirit prison are still held in spirit prison until their ordinance work is done. President Joseph F. Smith indicated that these spirits cannot be delivered from prison until "they have accepted the [gospel], *and* the work necessary to their redemption by the living be done for them" (*Gospel Doctrine,* 5th ed. [Salt Lake City: Deseret Book Co., 1939], p. 438, emphasis added).

President Joseph Fielding Smith taught that only after we have performed the ordinances in their behalf can the dead "receive the passport that entitles them to cross the gulf" (*Doctrines of Salvation,* comp. Bruce R. McConkie, 3 vols. [Salt Lake City: Bookcraft, 1954–56], 2:158).

President Spencer W. Kimball taught us the importance of participating in regular temple work. "Some of us have had occasion to wait for someone or something for a minute, an hour, a day, a week, or even a year. Can you imagine how our progenitors must feel, some of whom have perhaps been waiting for decades and even centuries for the temple work to be done for them?" ("The Things of Eternity—Stand We in Jeopardy?" *Ensign,* January 1977, p. 7.)

Following his remarks to the thief, Jesus turned his attention to the sorrowful scene of his mother, who despairingly stood at the foot of the cross. Jesus was concerned about her future welfare, for it appears as though Joseph had passed on and Mary's other sons had not yet joined the church of Jesus Christ. In order to make sure that she was associated with the Twelve and the Church, he requested that she be considered part of John the Beloved's family. He identified John and said to his mother, "Woman, behold thy son!" He then addressed John with the words, "Behold thy mother!" (John 19:26–27.) With these few words Jesus demonstrated his deep-seated love and concern for his mother and her welfare. He followed the commandment he had much earlier given from Mount Sinai: "Honour thy father and thy mother" (Exodus 20:12).

We seem to live at a time when many ignore this important commandment. In reference to our responsibility to parents as they become older, President James E. Faust said: "To honor parents certainly means to take care of physical needs. But it means much, much more. It means to show love, kindness, thoughtfulness, and concern for them all of the days of their lives. It means to help them preserve their dignity and self-respect in their declining years. It means to honor their wishes and desires and their teachings both before and after they are dead." ("Unwanted Messages," *Ensign,* November 1986, p. 9.)

We show love for our parents as we seek the Spirit and strive to do what is best for them and for our own immediate family. Since the needs of our parents vary, their needs can be met in a variety of ways. It may mean moving in with them or having them move in with us. They may need only financial help, or they may need us to visit several times a week and perform some of the tasks that have become too difficult for them to accomplish. They may just need our moral support and frequent visits, phone calls, or letters. As we strive to help our parents enjoy their golden years, we are following the example that Jesus set as he made arrangements for his mother from the cross.

The Savior's fourth statement from the cross has to do with the suffering he endured for our sins. President Marion G. Romney attempted to describe the extent of this suffering: "No man, nor set of men, nor all men put together, ever suffered what the Redeemer suffered in the Garden" ("The Atonement of the Savior," *Improvement Era,* December 1953, p. 942). Although this suffering started in Gethsemane, it was finished on the cross. It appears as though Jesus had to suffer for the sins of mankind completely alone, for his cry from the cross is, "My God, my God, why hast thou forsaken me?" (Matthew 27:46.)

Discussing this soul-piercing cry, Elder James E. Talmage wrote: "What mind of man can fathom the significance of that awful cry? It seems, that in addition to the fearful suffering incident to crucifixion, the agony of Gethsemane had recurred, intensified beyond human power to endure. In that bitterest hour the dying Christ was alone, alone in most terrible reality. That the supreme sacrifice of the Son might be consummated in all its fulness, the Father seems to have withdrawn the support of His immediate Presence, leaving to the Savior of men the glory of complete victory over the forces of sin and death." (*Jesus the Christ* [Salt Lake City: Deseret Book Co., 1973], p. 661.)

Now that Jesus has given us this wonderful gift of love, it is up to us to take advantage of it by truly repenting of our sins and turning our hearts and lives over to him and his gospel. Otherwise we will have to suffer even as he did (see D&C 19:16–19).

Once the needs of others had been taken care of, Jesus could now think of his own bodily needs. He cried out, "I thirst" (John 19:28). This attitude of putting God and others before his own personal needs is readily apparent throughout his life. His love for God and others was a major theme of his life and ministry. It was placing himself last that made him the extraordinary man that he was.

Placing God first in our lives will bring an order and direction to our lives that can be gained in no other way. President Ezra Taft Benson said: "When we put God first, all other things fall into their proper place or drop out of our lives. Our love of the Lord will govern the claims for our affection, the demands on our time, the interests we pursue, and the order of our priorities." ("The Great Commandment—Love the Lord," *Ensign,* May 1988, p. 4.)

The Savior's sixth and seventh statements from the cross refer to the successful completion of his assigned task and to his power over life and death. Because of his faithful obedience throughout his mortal ministry, he was able to say, "It is finished" (John 19:30). In effect Jesus was saying: "The job you sent me here to do is done. I lived a sinless life, and I suffered for the sins of all mankind. I organized the church of Jesus Christ here upon the earth, and I set a perfect example that others may follow. My work here is finished."

He then followed with his seventh and concluding statement, "Father, into thy hands I commend my spirit" (Luke 23:46). Because of the immortal nature of his Father and the mortal nature of his mother, he had in some unfathomable manner the ability to suffer death and the power to resurrect himself from the grave. In some incomprehensible way this made it possible for all of us to be resurrected.

Our goal should be that we, like Jesus, will be able to say at the end of our lives: "It is finished. What we came here to do has been accomplished." And what we came here to do is to *become* like God and help others do the same. We did not come here just to do good things but to become good. Joseph Smith stated that "if you wish to go where God is, you must be like God, or possess the principles which God possesses" (*Teachings of the Prophet Joseph Smith*, p. 216).

Through hundreds of correct choices made each day of our lives, we develop the attributes and character traits of God. This does not happen from merely going through the motions of obedience but from a complete commitment to the will of the Father. In Moroni 7:48 we are told that all those who are true followers of Christ will be like him when he comes. When our hearts are right and our motives are pure, doing will lead to becoming and we will fulfill the eternal purpose of our lives here.

Index

Parents, 111–12
Passover, 98
Paul, on fruits of the Spirit, 60
  on peace for doing good, 74
Peace, 14, 71, 72, 100–101
Persecution, 47–48, 56
Petersen, Mark E., on lying, 32
Pinegar, Rex D., on following
    Jesus' teachings, 64
  on priorities, 54
Pleasure, 21
Prayer, for blessings, 24, 94, 101
  to communicate with God, 28,
    61–62, 86
  for enemies, 45
  and fasting, 14
Premortal existence, 73
Pride, 27, 54, 55–56, 91
  and arrogance, 25, 34
Priesthood blessings, 14, 42–43
Priorities, 53–54
Promises, 35
Prophets, 28

— R —

Repentance, and baptism, 4, 23,
  after death, 110
  after sinning, 21, 104
Resurrection, 12
Revelation, personal, 6, 14, 24
Rey, Robert K., on service,
    96–97
Rigdon, Sidney, pride of, 26–27
Righteousness, 9
Ritchie, George G., story about
    World War II, 47–48

Romney, Marion G., on the
    Atonement, 112–13
  on following God's will, 13–14

— S —

Sacrament, 98, 102–7
Sacrifice, animal, 2
  things of the world, 57
Salvation, 43, 85
Scriptures, for guidance, 13, 85
  personal study of, 28, 96
  prophesies in, 15
Second Coming, 5–6
Self-evaluation, 28
Sermon on the Mount, 22, 45, 59
Service, 28, 36–37, 66, 96–97
  See also Church callings
Shepherds, 17–18
Sin, 20, 57, 94, 105
Smith, Joseph, on becoming like
    God, 114
  on dying young, 100
  on happiness, 21
  on things of God, 78
Smith, Joseph F., on forgiving
    enemies of Church, 45–46
  on loved ones and death,
    99–100
  on loving enemies and friends,
    46
  on spirit prison, 110–11
Smith, Joseph Fielding, on sacra-
    ment meeting, 103
  on temple ordinances, 111
Sorenson, Mollie, on testimony,
    61–62